The Value of Style in Fiction

This is the first book to demonstrate the v;
appreciative and interpretive in its "evalua
from Daniel Defoe through Jane Austen to   ., Charles Dickens
and Herman Melville to Don DeLillo and Toni Morrison. *The Value of Style in
Fiction* is designed not just for students and scholars of the English novel – and
its verbal "microplots" – but also for anyone interested in mastering the art of
the sentence by "writing along with" its finest exemplars in a fully descriptive
account: a stylistic challenge in its own right, exemplified by Stewart's
multifaceted critical modeling. Beginning with a state-of-the-field survey of
prose poetics, this manual of invested reading concludes with an "Inventory" of
terms (bolded throughout) drawn primarily from grammar, rhetoric, etymology,
and phonetics, but also narratology and poetic theory: a glossary whose
consultation can help cross-map certain verbal tendencies in literary-historical
evolution and its separate landmark writers.

Garrett Stewart is the James O. Freedman Professor of Letters at the University
of Iowa. After numerous books on fiction, poetics, film, and conceptual art,
his study of Victorian narrative style, *Novel Violence: A Narratography of
Victorian Fiction*, was awarded the 2011 Perkins Prize by the International
Society for the Study of Narrative. He is the author most recently of *The Deed of
Reading. Literature · Writing · Language · Philosophy* (2015) and *Transmedium:
Conceptualism 2.0 and the New Object Art* (2017), with a forthcoming volume
on the language of Dickens, entitled *The One, Other, and Only Dickens*. He was
elected in 2010 to the American Academy of Arts and Sciences.

The Value of Style in Fiction

Garrett Stewart
University of Iowa

CAMBRIDGE
UNIVERSITY PRESS

CAMBRIDGE
UNIVERSITY PRESS

University Printing House, Cambridge CB2 8BS, United Kingdom

One Liberty Plaza, 20th Floor, New York, NY 10006, USA

477 Williamstown Road, Port Melbourne, VIC 3207, Australia

314–321, 3rd Floor, Plot 3, Splendor Forum, Jasola District Centre, New Delhi – 110025, India

79 Anson Road, #06-04/06, Singapore 079906

Cambridge University Press is part of the University of Cambridge.

It furthers the University's mission by disseminating knowledge in the pursuit of education, learning, and research at the highest international levels of excellence.

www.cambridge.org
Information on this title: www.cambridge.org/9781107193857
DOI: 10.1017/9781108149976

First published 2018

Printed in the United Kingdom by Clays, St Ives plc

A catalogue record for this publication is available from the British Library.

ISBN 978-1-107-19385-7 Hardback

ISBN 978-1-316-64521-5 Paperback

Contents

I Introduction
Verbal Investments – Richness, Wealth, Value

One may speak of the *richness* of a sentence, the *wealth* of its invention, but *value* feels less metaphoric. Why – and, if so, how deployed here? In what relation to the thread and tread, the texture and pace, of words in their ordered but not ordained row? And what critical investments are implied by even starting with such questions? How will we end up wishing to posit the *worth* of style in the wording of single sentences by Austen or Hawthorne or Dickens or Conrad or Woolf? Or, more to the point: wanting to ask what *style is worth* in the work of analysis, as well as in the tenor of response?

Style is language in action. Accordingly, these chapters argue for the place of *prose* in our attention to *prose fiction*. Rescuing stylistic consideration of the English novel from an epoch of neglect, the book is intended for a cross section of literary readers interested in the nature and grain of fictional writing, with examples drawn from the whole history of British and American fiction, including the special translingual cases of Conrad and Nabokov. Yet the emphasis is not "authorial." Style is understood not as a "signature effect" but, instead, as a matter of literary ways and means. Emphasis falls not on the identifiable stylistic profile of one writer versus another, but rather on the stylistic registers that identify the work of writing in process, making its way and its meaning in words. And those registers are linguistic all the way down. It is a given of this study that broad exhibition of this point, over a wide array of writers and their fiction, can only help secure the claim. With ambitious prose, prose on the verbal stretch, one can dip in almost anywhere, from chosen writer to chosen novel. The question is only how deep – to what formative strata – that dip tends to reach.

The inaugural book in this Cambridge series, Peter Boxall's *The Value of the Novel*, is a study to whose phenomenological and cultural appraisal my volume would add the often-discounted measure of style on the ledger of assessment.[1] In his central chapter on "the Novel Body," Boxal stresses a kind of dialectic between represented somatic matter in the world of plot, on the one hand, whether the property of bodies or things, and, on the other hand, the presumed textual immateriality that conjures those entities in the mind's eye, "materializes" them sheerly as idea. This is how rendered characters, in particular, can be encountered both from outside and as if from within. Though not part of Boxall's investigation, one way in which style takes part in manifesting this interchange between "mere" writing and embodiment is when it makes palpable in reading – makes all but tangible – the phonic basis of verbal production in the silent but no less material enunciation (somaticized by readers themselves) of lexical forms and syntactic rhythms. In this way, the active engagement of our sensorium brings us closer to the imagined corporeal energy of fictional characters – across the conduit of style. On behalf of the very lives so described, we body forth what we read. Not all writing listens in on itself in this way. But much of the most intense and compelling does.

Though name recognition will inevitably attend many of the crisply immaculate or majestically exaggerated examples to come, or anything in between, the heavy weight of cited evidence does not bring this volume forward as an anthology of the greats, but rather as a meditation on the linguistic underpinnings of any such achievement. Examples are meant to contemplate not the style of geniuses but the very *genius of style*. From which emerges this abiding sense: that style is a quotient of literary writing, and so literary meaning, at its nearest point of readerly contact. It is the place where writing *takes*, wherever it thereby takes you, or however it takes you in – and thus out of yourself.

The interrogative starting point, time and again: style as opposed to what? As always, the sentence unit is the clearest litmus test in such investigation. But is the style of a given sentence as opposed to its meaning – its form over against what it formulates – a distinction without a difference? Two sides of the same coin? Students often have a hard time seeing otherwise, separating the two, noticing anything special about the former, or at least attempting to specify it. This book is meant to help. Why "style" per se, then? Or where exactly? As separable from what? No approach to the question can afford to ignore decades of literary theory that have refused all easy distinctions between form and content. That's exactly why style, once brought to the fore, can be recognized as so integral – even internal – to reading. Style is the constitutive first glimpse we have of a fictional scene – and this in either sense: setting or scenario, description or narrated action. Not least when deliberately bland and apparently transparent, style, from *stylus*, is where prose narrative makes its mark. And at its most ornate, involuted, or multifaceted, when manifestly less a window than a prism, style is still the only way "in" to the story – which only means the only way forward across the contour of prose fiction as prose. Even in refusing the outer/inner dyad of the form/content duality, Hayden White's productive inversion – in which he looked by title to "the content of the form" (the very inferences of structure in itself) – doesn't quite get us where we need to go in the matter of prose style.[2] Form is too formless, amorphous, or at best multivalent a term, as no less than a recent book on the topic, *On Form*, admits from the start.[3]

Nonetheless, even as the very question of form, variously defined, has been widely reopened in current literary study, style remains far from an "easy sell" in scholarly treatment. The very idea is often seen as too precious or belletristic, too author-centered rather than text-based, its study too appreciative in cast, even impressionist, certainly too windless in a world of urgencies other than verbal. Yet as understood, resuscitated, and sampled here, style is not a supplement or adjunct to narrative in prose fiction, some fetishized refinement of its literary form, but rather its operative vehicle: its almost tactile delivery system. Style is the discernible fictional energy of the prose itself, its level of pure invention – in effect, its fictionality in essence. Whatever its "value," it is not some elusive *value added*, relative in its worth from reader to reader. It's not what we get more of in Dickens than in Trollope, in James than in Dreiser.

Neither is it something that late Joyce, through travesty, transcends. Nor is it only the very difference between all such writers. It is the difference *within*: not just across and then between words kept in line by idea, but between the instated phrasing and its latent alternatives. As such, it locates an interplay of choices silenced but not entirely subsided as we read. Without lionizing the individual finesse or panache of a given writer, *reading for style* is always a reading for how a thing is said – and how it might have gone otherwise, and may sometimes still be shadowed in reception by that alternate possibility. Ultimately, such a reading is on the lookout, and on the listen, for what – by a particular string of words, understood as the active work of wording – a given passage may, above and beyond its meaning, be more intensively saying: in (just) so many words.

Any use of the blanket term *stylistics* for the "science" of style – as this nomenclature is often loosely applied – is divided in practice between *style analysis*, accounting for telltale "markers" in strictly linguistic terms apart from their interpretive pressure points, and *stylistic reading* in critical commentary, whose "closeness" starts simply with language on the way to inference. The latter habit is what gets developed and exercised here: a response that *reads the language* of fiction as well as through it – *through* in both senses, via and beyond. Hewing to worded sentences for their own phrasal cues, one grasps language's priority with no need to overstate or romanticize its magic. Style is disclosure, yes; style is revelation; but no literary epiphany implied. There is simply nowhere else to look, nothing else to listen to – or for. Style is the material objectification in words of so-called subject matter.

Whether stripped down or elaborated, stringent or florid, ironic or ecstatic, style is the Writing behind the written – and, precisely in this charged sensitivity to the either/or of manner, ranging from broad dichotomies of stance and tone down to the least ambivalence of syntax. On this understanding, prose style is the feature of writing that exceeds all limiting characterizations – high or low, classic or rococo, serene or tortured – in the close-grained work of novelist execution: the *sine qua non* of sequence itself. Stylistic analysis, then, is not concerned either with nit-picking or with pecking orders of appreciation – either with fussy technical discriminations or with broad adjudications of the bespangled versus the pellucid, the high versus the plain, you name it. Nor, within a single sentence, is style relegated for notice to the salient or deviant effect only, rather than the systematic and normative. For comparison, it is fair to say that the topic of these pages is as far from the showy "stylings" of interior design as it is, at the other end of the spectrum, from the normative standards of a press's "house style." In the heat of reading, style is precisely that quality of literary experience undecidable in advance, pitched to the descriptions it materializes, timed to the narrative motions it propels.

All this might well be granted, of course, without necessarily igniting scholarly (or student) interest. This is because the value of style, certainly its academic "exchange value," depends in part, in any one moment of discussion, on the styles of valuation by which fiction is addressed – or, more to the point, on the styles of attention to which it is submitted: political, theoretical, ideological, cognitive, what have you. So let it be said up front. For too long, style has been the deviance, or say the insistent evidence, that dare not speak its name. In prose fiction, it is the marked work of language too easily suppressed in critical remark. Bracketing its distractions, however, only ignores their real task. Either veering from or aggressively cementing neutral verbal norms and, in so doing, diverging from mere function into highlighted *effect*, style may at times seem to be riding in on the back of story – while actually carrying it forward. But even consensus on that latter point of priority, when achieved in certain theoretical circles, hasn't necessarily bred renewed commitment. There are hopeful signs, though – besides the interest of Cambridge University Press in such a volume – including an international symposium held at the University of New South Wales in December of 2017 that focused, among other questions of prose style, on why the academic discipline of "stylistics" (broadly conceived) has had so little traffic with prose, and especially with prose narrative, in its gravitation to the metered verse of poetry – and where, correctively, we might take discussion instead. One answer (suggested in my keynote address there, and as fleshed out in Chapter 2): back to where we've been in the assessed legacy of prose fiction, but revisiting the terrain more attentively from the verbal ground up. And with another question always in mind: how *literary* is such critical examination to be?

Even former if sporadic partnerships between a thematic and a stylistic analysis of fiction in the New Critical moment have, in disciplinary terms, been mostly dissolved in recent (post-"critical"?) discussion under the motive of critique.[4] The very protocols of verbal consideration, as in the study of poetry as well, have seen a resulting steep decline. Indeed, rather in the mode of those mass-marketed guides "For Dummies" in an age of atrophied verbal instincts, Terry Eagleton's bluntly titled *How to Read a Poem*, followed by *How to Read Literature*, famously bemoaned the fate of old-fashioned, honest-to-goodness literary criticism – as if in unsaid recantation of his own career-long theoretical and political agenda for his Marxist understanding of literary works.[5] For Eagleton, the "dying art" of criticism, in its foundational mode of close reading, has gone the way of "thatching or clog dancing" (*Poem*, 1). No surprise that literary instruction in such methods now comes forth from him in a rough-and-ready DIY mode, since its goals and techniques are rarely taught these days in a formal academic setting. In the same spirit, given its heyday in the 1950s and 1960s, one could well say that the specific procedures of stylistic reading (in its interpretive if not strictly linguistic venues) have waned at least as decisively – suffering the fate, if not of clog dancing, at least of the mimeograph and the mono hi-fi.

But wait. Those particular analogies of mine, I realized just after drafting, have an etymological as well as a historical resonance with literary style: this, in their association with textual impress ("graph") as well as, mixing metaphors, in their "one-speaker" fidelity of tone. That's style for you, springing the pertinent afterthought: not necessarily premeditated, but legible after the fact. For my drafted phrasing accidentally helps emphasize that there is, under the sign of style, some potent convergence of the mimetic, the graphic, and the phonic. This is why the continued inestimable value (there, I've said it!) of attending to style in fiction seeks clarification in such a volume as this by recognizing what is indeed a double audio/visual dimension in the language *on* which – and in a complementary sense *by* which – the idea of style trains perception. Yes, *mimeography* plus monaural *fidelity*. What is sprung from this conjunction is a reminder about the activation of written text. Attention comes fully alive in the reading of fiction when prose is understood not just as *graphing* (tracing out) style's unique inflections of the *mimetic* impulse, but as keeping *faith*, in the sense of an enunciated "fidelity," with the fundamental *aural* undertone of phonetic language in process.

From thatching to fax machines to PDFs: times do change. Certainly "scanning" a poem for analysis is more likely these days to imply its email attachment for a class than any metrical deliberation expected when the group next convenes. More so, and more to the point, except for casual mention in journalistic reviews, whether positive or negative, style as a factor in the reading of prose fiction has suffered an even worse academic fate than scansion or metaphoric analysis in the study of verse. Students don't even know it's gone missing from their toolkits. I must have realized, even at the time, that I was mishearing, grasping at straws – victim of an almost literary pun – when I thought I understood a doctoral student of English I happened to meet recently, in response to my initial curiosity about his scholarly interests, to be planning "a diction theory of Victorian fiction." Really? My own energized uptake was quickly exposed as mistaken. "Oh, no, no: addiction theory – you know, in light of disability and precarity studies." One does know. But, apart from the skills of that particular student, what "a diction study" might constitute would mostly elude at least two or three generations of his peers.

In and beyond such cross-lexical ambiguity as accidentally triggered in that brief scholarly chat, the volatility of diction is very much part of the picture in this book: word choice itself, from sentence to sentence, rather than just its showcasing in the celebrated wordsmiths of literary history. This is diction in the sense not of *usage* (proper or substandard; high or low) but of kinetic *use*: the lexicon in motivated requisition, vocabulary in process – widely varying, of course, from writer to writer, period to period. And never reduced to the merely *useful*. Nor to the privately favored. Process is the issue here, not preference. Certainly any reader's authorial druthers go to the back of the queue in this line of investigation. Before "the style" (generalized often beyond specification) that one cottons to more in this novelist than in that, from one century or the next, lies the stylistic texture one has necessarily processed in reading the prose of either writer. Style is not some incidental consideration or predilection. It is the medium of all transmitted incident. It is thus properly a branch of media study – and as much a prey to noise in the channel as any other mode of signal transfer.

Indeed, thinking of style in this way may offer one route toward a revitalized attention to its services and seductions in an age of media theory and even digital humanities – if perhaps through the back door. So an anecdote here – and something of a literary-critical parable, drawn from that halfway house between poetry and prose known as Shakespearean theater. The literary (and in fact, if intermittently, stylistic) critic, Franco Moretti, more influential lately for his computer-programmed "distant reading," recently headed up an experiment at the Stanford Literary Lab (the flaunted scientific name constituting an oxymoron only to the uninitiated) to tackle the greatest writer of all, though on other grounds than the writing – at least to begin with. The investigation was designed – just the right word, by computer software – to inquire into the mappable schemata of character interaction and dialogic patterning in *Hamlet*, doing so by number-crunching a tabulation of who speaks to whom. Finding in the process that only Horatio has encounters with everybody, Moretti wanted then to know, to be reminded, of what Horatio actually sounds like in those exchanges. For a methodological essay in *New Left Review*, he thus shelves for the moment his statistical results and goes back to the play itself in its unsifted form – on page rather than spreadsheet – engaging in this way with the raw data, as it were, of its style.[6] Which means reading it up close after all. And which in this case means discovering that Horatio (quite unlike Charles Altieri's Claudius, discussed below) wields the least colorful, least imaginative, least figurative language in the play. Based on this flatness, this leveling, this predominant intermediation rather than expressive or rhetorical bent, Moretti can venture an eye-opening amalgam of "symptomatic" political reading and historicist "discourse analysis" sieved through the filters of style. For what he thus finds in Horatio's talk – in the character's telltale and world-historical role as ubiquitous communication circuit more than effus-ing subject – is nothing less than the birth of state discourse (and thus eventually of modern and faceless bureaucratese itself) out of the gradually outmoded flights of aristocratic rhetoric and its privi-leged stylizations.

In Buffon's "Discourse on Style" from well into the next cen-tury after Shakespeare, we hear – in the mode of celebration – that "style is the man himself." If so, Horatio's dialogue is that of a dep-ersonalized state functionary. The methodological allegory here, as Moretti might well be inclined to agree: that one of the best tests of the digital enterprise is the determination of its own limits. And so, too, with style: one among its many registers is the moment when it is dialed down almost to zero. In Horatio's case, the results are resonant in their very neutrality. Style isn't the man so much as the embryonic manifestation of a broader discursive regime. But interpretation needs to be called in to assess his speech as such. The enterprise of "corpus stylistics" notwithstanding, style in its full operation can't be tabulated; it can only be *read*. And, as suggested above, the corpus in question in this respect, when encountering the play outside of its impersonation on stage, is the sounding-board of each reading body in silent intake – and uptake.

Verbal mediation is every bit as telling in the language of fic-tion as in Shakespeare's dramatic verse or its interleaved prose, both in a given text and in the tacit evolution of such fictional discourse over time. Once there was the dutiful mimesis of Robinson Crusoe on his island in the first years of English fiction, just taking things up, or setting them down, by hand and word alike. His was a para-documentary prose traced by modernist critic Hugh Kenner, in retro-spect, as positing the material condition of "one-word-per-thing" in the manner of a recipe for reconstructed event.[7] From there, the genre moved through two fertile centuries of fictional practice devoted in part to perfecting, from Jane Austen to Toni Morrison and beyond, the subjectivist flexibilities of free indirect discourse. Think of such channelings of consciousness in Austen (here the heroine's amorous nostalgia in meeting her former fiancé Wentworth again years later in *Persuasion*) as "Once so much to each other! Now nothing! There *had* been a time…" This very mode of poetic license has, in turn, induced considerable recent debate over its rhetorical and political implications in a cultural logistics of invaded privacy. Style can be conduit and culprit alike. Continuing in a longer transformation (to be little more than glanced at, given its complexity, in Chapter 2) between mock-document and subjective proxy, Defoe to Austen, the trajectory of prose style arrives two centuries later at what one might call the free indirect optics of reported "sightings" clicked past in the narrative armature of contemporary drone novels. Yet again, point of view is everything.

And once more style articulates the perspectival measure of event, the register of tone, and the inner topography of response. That is why Stanley Fish, years back, could claim his readings of grammatical waver in Milton, and the performed fall into post-Edenic ambiguity, as an "affective stylistics."[8] Given a certain fitful resurgence of formal response over the last decade and a half or so (in potential league, as is often suggested, with "affect theory"), we have come round to something more like a rhetoric of affect than an affective stylistics – but not programmatically verbal (or textual) in its attentions. Neoformalism, arising conterminously with the so-called "affective turn" (while scarcely identified as a second wind for Fish's original approach), is the usual designator of choice for a reading putatively recommitted to formal literary categories – though it is often shunted away from phrasing itself to questions of meter in poetry, or genre in fiction, with very little sentence-by-sentence attention to diction, syntax, metaphor, and the rest.

Why not? What would have sent such obvious literary issues into so thorough a retreat – and so long a publishing silence – that even a rejuvenated formalist rallying cry would be slow to take renewed aim at them? Why would the most recent book devoted explicitly to the topic of literary style hail from the precincts of linguistics, not literary study, and date from as far back as 1981?[9] As surprising as this sounds when the question is put rhetorically, the answers are hardly far to seek. As if resulting in a sudden vacuum at the eye of a hurricane, a scholarly perfect storm – of several decades' escalating duration – has certainly sucked the wind from the sails of stylistic reading.

Given its common (if narrow) understanding as a signature effect of incomparable literary talent, marked out as the branded "style" of this author or that, it was no surprise that the canon-busting juggernaut against unassailable masterworks would take its toll on stylistic considerations. In this reaction against an authorial privilege entrenched in its bastions of dominant gender, race, class, and metropolitan centrality, combined with the "Death of the Author" verdict of French theory (in Roland Barthes and Michel Foucault especially) – elevating *textuality* per se over its local execution by one writer or another – it was all but inevitable that traditional stylistics would have been swept aside. When also downplayed by the historicist emphasis on texts as the sampling of cultural discourse rather than the exercise of inventive writing – and then sidelined in turn by an identity politics that has rendered a collective cultural voice of more primacy than individual gestures of expression,[10] and perhaps suffering an extra taint inherited from the spreading pop vernacular of "lifestyle," a watery grave for stylistics seemed all but assured amid the sea changes of the profession. And you'd certainly be right to think that the various theorists of the posthuman in these same years have had little interpretive truck with the tacit anthropocentrism of "the stylist" – even in a gender-corrected "style is the person" mode.

Whatever the causes, another Miltonist since Fish has more recently pushed back against the notion of such obsolescence. He has done so in venturing – as if once more into the widening breach – an explicitly *literary* criticism in its three determining facets. For Gordon Teskey, these are philology, poetics, and aesthetics – involving, respectively, description, interpretation, and judgment or appraisal (the last a matter of evaluation in the everyday sense, however concerted and erudite, as contrasted with the strictly typological sense in Roland Barthes, to be explored shortly).[11] Pursuing the logic of his triad, Teskey notes that to account for what is actually going on in complex poetry can be harder to accomplish than it might seem, thus justifying the disciplinary status of such expertise. Indeed, though it is often more demanding than a comparable glossing of narrative prose, with Milton being even more complicated than the Miltonic Melville – it is in no greater degree a matter of style. For when understood as more fully imbricated with theme than are the underspecified prompts to "surface reading"[12] opted for in recent calls for such a return to manifest or immanent (rather than ideologically encrypted) inference, style comes clear as the surest guide to the underlying "poetics" (Teskey again) of entire works – as well as of the separate sentences that prosecute them.

Suffice it to say, further, that the final phase in this threefold task of the critic is not any more rigidly compartmentalized than its preparatory obligations. Judgments of worth have usually been achieved already in the appreciated interplay between the power of phrase and the structure of vision. And if so, the philology of stylistic attention has been their spur. The "value of John Milton" is there, in short, as much in his orotund Latinate syntax and phonetic density as in his prophetic transfiguration of Latin literary models. And, to anticipate the next phase of our discussion, the sonorous thunder of Miltonic cadence cannot be reduced to the oral dictation of his verse under the curse of blindness. The tones of Miltonic harmonies, both tonic and dominant, are heard on the page as well.

I allude to this last misleading temptation, about oral primacy in the rhythmic energies of the blind bard, for its place in a larger debate – and a further theoretic crisis for stylistic reading: a setback often misleading in its own terms, and still with us decades later. Here is another constraint imposed on any full-throated philological conversation. For when style is advanced beyond linguistic determinations – and hence mystified, as it still tends implicitly to be in the agendas of creative writing pedagogy, as the Voice of the writer – every poststructuralist allergy to the language of "presence," to Logos as embodiment, kicks in. And rightly. I had no problem, as we say, just some terminological trouble, in making sure that my 1990 book on the "phonotext" of literary language in both prose and poetry, *Reading Voices*, was understood to be titled (and entitled thereby to its claims) only as a clause, not a phrase.[13] Reading alone voices the language of literature. Twenty-five years later, as one of the most theoretically suggestive and methodologically promising works in a neoformalist vein, David Nowell Smith's *On Voice in Poetry: the Work of Animation* is still obliged to make clear that "work" isn't a stable noun of imputed lifelike vivacity in the animated literary object.[14] "Work" names, rather, the ongoing labor of production that instigates – through the rhythm of meter especially, in Smith's view – the cadence of oral enunciation (not the timbre of a wired authorial presence) from a nonetheless definitively silent page. Suffice it to say that I'll be recording, in what follows, not the stylistic Voices of Austen or Melville or D. H. Lawrence but the signals of their textual voicings – or what Steven Connor has recently called, in connection with Samuel Beckett's fiction, and with overtones of "white noise," a "writing" of "the white voice" in the reader's own internal sounding of inscribed text.[15] To this extent only, the gag order on voicing in high theory needs lifting.

In something of a similar spirit, for his commentary *How Novels Work*, John Mullan gives pride of place, in his chapter on "Style," to the question of "tone" – while also being well aware that the very term suffers from guilt-by-overassociation with autonomous Voice (capital V) under a deconstructive critique.[16] Fending off such objections to an audiocentric bias, his subdivided topics – after a distinction between "plain" and "antique" tonalities of style – range across the varied effects of parataxis, paragraphing, diction, amplification, parentheses, hyperbole, pastiche, heteroglossia, and streams of consciousness, all as contributing in different ways to "tone." I intend the present volume's further emphasis on something like phonetic *intonation* as a complement to these and other structuring determinations of prose fiction in the manner, and linguistic matter, of its prose as such.

So far in recent critical discourse, it must be said, the specific claims for a recuperative neoformalism have been of little moment in resuscitating anything one might call stylistic analysis in fiction – even when these claims are advanced under the dubious banner of a "surface reading" staged to resist a former "hermeneutics of suspicion," with its imputed tendency to dissipate the texture of writing into the mere ideological traction of its unwritten assumptions. For one thing, the polemical backlash in favor of surface over symptom is not often linked to anything terribly specific in the skein and contour of such a championed outward plane of meaning. And for another, this polemic tends to forget or ignore the fact that the best work in the annals of "symptomatic reading" – as most influentially prosecuted by Fredric Jameson (as well as early Moretti) – tests for its symptoms (as the metaphor would imply) precisely *on* the surface. Where else? The method is hobbled by no blindness to immanent form, which is registered precisely as an index to those "suspicious" cultural or aesthetic premises that are then probed for their "cognitive horizons" or the deep structures of their "political unconscious."[17]

Furthermore, in the name of "surface reading," a resistance to the structural depth charges of skeptical critique also tends to miss the fact that the literary surface is not some encrustation of verbal texture on which the analytic lens can be steadily focused, but rather a laminated and layered thing in itself, with its own density and pulse to consider: just the thing that's still repeatedly minimized, especially in the reading of prose. Whatever the hermeneutic yield might be if pursued, it certainly seems fair (if I may disinfect the term) to *suspect* that, in complex writing, more is going on than meets the eye at first pass – going on, and going into what we do immediately notice: when our attention operates, that is, at the surface of phrasing itself. That more is in part the intensification brought, wrought, by style – and impacting the reading moment more deeply, beneath any mere surface, by the very weight and force of its articulation. It is this stylistic quotient that is ignored at peril of lost power in the inference of phrase – and certainly of forestalled explanation in any account of such phrasing's internal engineering. To put such objections at their most obvious: what may appear on the surface of the page is the line of words; the *wording* is something else – not simply visible, imprinted. Wording is the activated infrastructure of meaning: not only prior to the word array as processed, as read, but a formative dynamic recovered in the very act of reading.

Stylistic marginalization aside in particular reading practices, however, the fact of style remains – not as a detachable and certified object of study on its own, but as a perceptible ingredient of fiction. And more: as part of its literary fundament. Aside from appraisal per se, as in a "distinguished master of English prose," it should be remembered that style, conceived over against anything else on the novelistic page, is after all – to this extent a student's naïve response is correct – a distinction without a difference. It can't be peeled away, either in abstraction or concrete detail, from the local description it constitutes. The term "form," seen in this light, is a more complete abstraction than "style," the former term quite shapeless without specification. Often lost sight of, this distinction between form and its subset in style, though not needing to be policed, is still much worth bearing in mind. Some system other or larger than the verbal braid of a given prose passage may, yes, *form* or *inform* it. Style, instead, is a name for the reader's *passage through it*, narrative's only *way forward*. Form, then, can have a transitive effect on style. Except for the trending grammar of popular usage, though, as in the lingo of fashion or design or real estate presentation, style isn't a verb at all. It subsists and resides, as articulation itself, rather than dictates or organizes. Not a verb – except in the nonlinguistic and reflexive sense, of course: "those ambitious students *style* themselves creative writers." In the literary event of actual creative writing, however, style, as contrasted with certain formal pressures, does not operate *on*; it inheres in.

So how to take its measure and mine its very depths, rather than mistaking them for a surface? Despite, or because of, his famous claim for the "Death of the Author" in the midwifing of text by cultural conditioning, Barthes is still, always, a generative place to start. His incremental approach in *S/Z* breaks up the Balzac text under consideration into hundreds of legible units, which he terms "lexias."[18] These are the smallest units of legibility, of reading – but dubbed as such with no particular interest in the lexical or syntactical structure of Balzac's own writing, its internal build of sound into sense – except at certain anomalous moments of saturated cultural assumptions in a received turn of phrase. To say so is to note that, in stressing the coded structure of Balzac's prototypical realism, Barthes sustains a linguistic model, but not a linguistic focus. His interest is in the grammar of narrative, rather than in narrative grammar. What emerges is a massive contribution to narratology and reader-response theory, yet exposing more the modular than the molecular nature of the constructed fiction.

In all this, what ends up surprising students of his work – as he traces out the effects of precoded assumptions in the weave of the "realist" illusion across one of his lexias after another – is that the "stereography" of this textual world building is summed up as if it were a stereophony. This occurs when one imagined Voice after another is understood as speaking forth the codes, as in the Voice of Science (culture) or the Voice of the Person (not the speaking voice of either character or narrator, but instead the articulatory mechanism, the loom of interwoven assumptions, by which characters are spun into credible presence by prose).[19] For Barthes, of course, such multiple Voices lay bare the illusion of a discursive Authority behind the authored verbal effects. For us, with an adjusted focus on the actual shaping of phrase, the Voice of constructed meaning is a metaphor (that, and nothing more) for style – and all the more pertinent when part of what it depends on is the frequent sound play of syllabic sequences.

By contrast with Barthes's practice, in what I suggested above as a modular rather than a molecular reading, my own theoretical work in **"narratography"** – directed most recently, in *The Deed of Reading*, at the microstructures of fictional prose as prose *friction* – has been meant to supplement such an exhaustive semiotics as we find in Barthes: to fill in, even beneath the high-voltage radar of his scrutiny, those phrasal increments and intervals that make worded sentences before making narrative sense.[20] Prose operates in this way by the steady fabrication of plot – again, from the ground up, in various armatures of its infrastructure – through the very allotment of syllables. Such are the constituent verbal impulses, along with broader-scale effects, that an emphasis on style will put forward in this volume. Among the many things that the Marxist in Barthes is famous for claiming is "that a little formalism turns one away from history, but that a lot brings one back to it."[21] The corollary here: a foray or two into verbal analysis may seem to detach you from the narrative mainsprings of a particular fiction, but enough stylistic reading embeds you in them again. Where you are always hearing things.

This is exactly the crucial interface of style that gets minimized in the most influential definition of narrational process, at least for screen studies. David Bordwell has scrupulously pursued the much-investigated narratological dyad of discourse versus story – back, first, to Aristotle's *Poetics*, and then on down through the formalist lineage to arrive at this crucial distinction between narration (the act) and narrative (the delivered, which is to say manifested, story): "Narration is the process whereby *syuzhet* plus style collaborate in cueing and channeling the viewer's construction of the *fabula*."[22] To paraphrase (while substituting, readily enough, reader for viewer), the textual "fable" at stake isn't already on hand, waiting to be packaged by a chosen literary form (*syuzhet*). Only structure "plus style" can induce in the reader a sense of the story, which response has thus coproduced in the act of construing it. Though subordinated to broader formal patterns by the mere add-on status of "plus," the understanding of "style" in the filmic scope of Bordwell's definition gravitates, basically, to cinematographic and editorial *technique*. And one might therefore insist, *contra* Bordwell, or at least one level down from his emphasis, that only technique articulates the structure by which the story comes before us. The supplement (the "plus") is in fact the generative engine. So, for our purposes, style in fiction *structures the very manner in which narration enlists us in constructing the narrative*. Granted, story doesn't precede and find shape in its structuration but is only precipitated from it by way of a cognitive process one could call audience participation. In a related vein, this is why the evidence to come will suggest that style is not a final inflection of content but the sheer possibility – and the present energy – of its composite manifestation in words.

Style, then, is not the last refinement of meaning but its articulating energy from the start. That's why processes we might wish to collect under a rubric like "the structuring of prose" would involve the medium of fiction as both subject and object of literary *formation*: the shaping labor of language as well as its resultant *formulations*.

This becomes all the clearer if we move to restate the case in terms of the **poetic function** from structural linguistics: a function that organizes its own defining poesis (internal patterning) while ordering larger sentence spans. Indeed, Roman Jacobson's work in structural poetics hovers everywhere in the background of Barthes's *S/Z*.[23] Ingrained cultural assumptions, returning at intervals across the build of Balzac's narrative – and so stacking up in response – form a kind of vertical axis, on Barthes's account, not unlike (he might have added) the very column of **phonemic** or lexical selection in linguistics. In language, in speech, pertinent differences between a single letter and its "functional equivalent" as phonemic increment (*r* versus *l* in that last word's near miss of "inclement," for instance), selected from the verbal stack of alphabetic alternatives for a given syllabic slot, make for differences as fundamental as that between the choice of a pronoun or a noun – She or Sheila, say – to begin a sentence (and perhaps a story). Predication follows, based on similar choices at each stage of horizontal advance along the syntactic line. But if the narratable fact that Sheila breaks up with her lover Frederick has been formatted instead as "Sheila sheds Freddy" – or, in Jakobson's example from the 1950s bumper sticker, if the quiet **assonance** of "I'm for Eisenhower" flowers into the pop poetry of "I Like Ike" (358) – then the "poetic function" has been engaged, as prominent in advertising as it is in Romantic verse.

That function begins, by famous definition, in "the projection of the principle of equivalence" – by which Jakobson means the maximizing of *comparability* in forward iteration (with "like" chosen over "support," for instance, in that political slogan's verb column, just as "I" is chosen over "We," for further assonance, from among first-person pronoun options, singular versus plural). What takes place, in a kind of serial displacement, is the "projection" of a strictly structural "principle of equivalence" (principle in the abstract) "from the axis of selection to the axis of combination": from word choice to syntax, or, we might say, from initial decision to succession. In the build of the sentence, the linguistic model of clearly parallel options, when spaced out as partial iterations, is found generating more comparability, more sameness or equivalence, than sheer sequence needs – or, in other words, engendering "metaphoric" likeness across the space of sheer grammatical accumulation. Leading flashpoints for Jakobson are meter, as well as assonance and alliteration ("I Like Ike"), each commonly found in the extra-semantic imposition ("projection") of *marked* form upon sentence formation. Less dependent on strict recurrence, but no less on perceived selection, style invites definition in just these terms: the recognized projection of alternatives, still cognitively viable, onto a chosen sequence, where the idea of equivalence may come across, instead, if only incidentally in certain cases, as equivocation or duality. Or put it this way: style is a verbal combination still shadowed with its own founding options – and thrown into relief by them. Once again, we note how the structuring at once *of* and *by* style addresses not just the internal molding of phrase but the shaping work that prose, all told, exerts upon idea.

The "poetic function" in Jakobson certainly helps isolate and identify many a stylistic feature in prose. But this book owes a more specific "poetic" allegiance, even debt, to a work like Christopher Ricks's *The Force of Poetry* than to most commentaries on prose fiction. That force is, for Ricks, an inertial momentum in the verse itself, its enjambments, its prepositional subordinations, its phrasal torsion and drive. It is a force inherent in the writing – and appreciable *ad hoc* from passage to passage. Force: not in the honorific rhetorical sense of "forceful," but ingrained in the build and vectoring of linguistic texture. It is according to this sense of force that one is able to capture certain intertwined aspects of prose style as well. Some of these are subdivided in their leading features in the ten-step program of renovated attention next sketched out across a single, organically branching sentence claiming a freestanding paragraph of its own.

So it is that a move from the cross-sectioned *sounds and syllables* (1) building up the fiber, timber, and tone of diction in the special *lexicon* (2) of a given text is only a first step on the way, regardless of the situated *tense* (present, past, future) of the represented action (transitive, intransitive, passive) or scene (3), toward the pieced-out time and pace of meaning known as *syntax* (4), abetted in progress by the seemingly most negligible fixtures of prepositions and conjunctions, with this threadwork (and tacit channeling) of action serving in turn, according to the embraced or flouted constraints of grammar, to dispose and array whatever *figural language* (5) may well be put into counterpoint with the cited idioms of human *figures in dialogue* (6), with each level of language (attributed or not) being organized, now separately, now together, in patterns of repetition and variation exceeding mimesis (sheer representation) under the force of prose *poesis* in the Jakobsonian sense (7) – and thereby found not only arcing across whole syntactic structures but concentrated as well in the narrower phonic *play* of inter-animated words and word sounds (8), puns included, even as any such recursive or self-doubling increments of depiction contribute to fictional perspectives that are *focalized* (9) either through delegated characters or via a sponsoring omniscience nuanced and rerouted by varying degrees of *free indirect discourse* (10), including its modernist legacy in stream of consciousness, all as part of an uncanny access to worlds in words.

All told: ten recurrent generators, often intrinsically marked by recurrence itself, that might have been accorded (and cordoned off as) separate chapters, but that stay truer to the effects of style in action when their frequent complementarity and interpenetration are respected in analysis. I strain attention with that tenfold roundup, not just for a concentrated and cross-mapped preview of the broad categories of effect most often tested out below, but because – eliciting something of a syntactic enactment in its own right – such a sentence anticipates how much the effects at stake in the forthcoming chapters are indeed not just collaborative but regularly overlapped, dovetailed, simultaneous, or otherwise inextricable. Imitative syntax, then: my deliberately distended and overtaxed attempt at tensile give, slippage, and comprehension all at once. We are certainly to see many other such attempts, far more elegant and gripping, in the prose waiting to be sampled (including two tautly compressed sentences still to come in this Introduction, from the very different modernists, Joseph Conrad and Virginia Woolf). As it happens, style is often closely timed to reported action in just this sense – but only as a special case of a general principle.

As it happens? Better: style is *where* it happens – where the action is – carrying its own narrative charge even while ferrying the plot. That is its value: as primary valence of the literary event. In all the usual dichotomies that gird, grid, and filter a reader's perception of narrative – where discussion turns repeatedly on the issue of discourse versus story, structure versus reported event, telling and told – style is, again, the Writing of all things written. In appreciating this sense of an underlying impetus or drive rather than a mere structural toolkit, technical terms taken up in the appended Inventory will be held to a minimum in their cross-referenced glossing, dispensed (by bolding) in the chapters themselves on a need-to-know basis. Even armed with them for precision's sake, response needs to remain intuitive in order to catch the rhetorical spirit of the literary letter. Retaining the hermeneutic instinct from the agendas of close reading, but with an eye to the production rather than the recognition of semantic or psychological patterns in the shaping of phrase, stylistic reading is therefore a *deep* reading: its effects rendered legible only against the fund of latent linguistic options, in grammar and vocabulary, from which a given effect is, in the traditional (and nonpolemic) sense, *surfaced*. Deep reading (always more than skindeep, even when attending to the likes of fleeting syllabic patterns as structuring forces) remains uniquely open in this way to the propulsive mutations of wonder – and delight. When Dickens introduces us in *Bleak House* (1853), for instance, to "a pink, fresh-faced, crisp-looking gentleman with a weak voice, white teeth, light hair, and surprised eyes," the most striking feature – facial and stylistic – emerges from the previous run of monosyllabic descriptors. This happens when noting the three-syllabled clincher that compounds the abutted assonance of "white" with "light" by the echoic double bulge of "surpr*ised* *eyes*." Pried open from an epithet in search of its noun, such a final turn of phonetic phrase is nothing less than a sight for sore ears. And, come to think of it, something of a phrasal surprise in its own mimic right. What the prose turns of Conrad, next, or later of Woolf, end up performing, however, is a clearer syntactic mirror of sequential thematic sense.

Since style will ultimately find its fullest definition as well as demonstration – through instanced principle – in more of such illustrations to come, it's only apt to let fictional ruminations on the matter of meaning's manifestation, in self-exampling turns of phrase, help lead us forward at the outset. Let me borrow, then, with a certain license for adjustment, a benchmark formulation of aesthetic intent, ratcheting it down from a question of meaning to one of phrasing. Famously for the narrator, Marlow, in Joseph Conrad's *Heart of Darkness* (1899), "the meaning of an episode was not inside like a kernel but outside, enveloping the tale which brought it out only as a glow..." An emergent glow rather than an energized core? Forgive the temporary cheat; the sentence actually rolls straight on, the momentary *phrase* of simile actually triggering a whole *clause* of reoriented subordination: "... only as a glow brings out a haze, in the likeness of one of these misty halos that sometimes are made visible by the spectral illumination of moonshine."[24] This maxim of interpretation is of course a stylistic feat of legerdemain in itself. The all-but-reversible gestalt of that phrasing – which, like a poetic enjambment, would be complete enough at "only as a glow" – then switches grammar so that the glow issues in a penumbral "haze": the afterglow of narrative event in its interpretable aura. Indeed, the visual stress here (in this version of "affective stylistics" for fictional prose) is so insistent that the summoned effect isn't just "like" but "in the likeness of" the echoic "halos." Likeness would, of course, seem the whole point: sheer figure. The sun has just set on the Thames, with no mention of moonlight, only stars coming out – yet the "halo" trope is strangely "one of these," not those, as if such an phenomenon were, in more than metaphoric form, already in the mind's eye of the embodied narrator. Which, no doubt, it is – and in immediate transference to the reader.

Haze or halo: which to choose, which to use first, and then how to space out the long-voweled *lo* between "glow" and "halo"? How much immediacy should be instilled, even a bit illogically, with that chosen demonstrative adjective, "these" over "those"? And, anyway, should storytelling be taking itself as its own topic like this, in some kind of reflexive antecedence (these images right here), and thereby taking its own interpretive temperature? In reading, the latent force of such reconstructed authorial questions, such auto-valuation, is part of the stylistic effect. By adjusted analogy with Conrad's trope, then, we might want to say that style is not the wrapper or packaging of import, husk to its kernel, but rather the very thing that *brings it out*: again its vehicle, its transmission, however spectral at times in its own right.

As part of a hazy penumbra in the orbit of meaning, such is style's sometimes ineffable "worth" – its worth in the throes of consideration. It's a word used by Nathaniel Hawthorne, too, in a curious phonetic loop of self-affirming ratification at the stylistic level. Speaking of the vicissitudes of the Pyncheon lineage in *The House of the Seven Gables* (1851), he writes: "Were these to be worthily recounted, they would form a narrative of no small interest and instruction, and possessing, moreover, a certain remarkable unity, which might almost seem the result of artistic arrangement."[25] Trouble is, there would be way too much to read. So the chronicler's dream of synoptic unity must go by the board, but not without proof that our present narrator would be, if anyone, just the man for this job. For the style of his own conditional grammar, about the value of such recorded lineage, has already been proven in its own "remarkable" internal "unity" by an ephemeral crossword echo that has internalized "worth-i-ly" in the very grammar of its conjectural mood in "were the-se." From the ground up, yet again, the build-up of sounds and syllables is made obliquely apparent.

Pointed up by the first of many such phonetic pressure points we will come upon in examples ahead, sometimes springing semantic leaks rather than just internal echoes, generalization is invited. Such, indeed, is the "worth" of style, and its value too – and the latter at least as much in the sense of "artistic arrangement" (Hawthorne's term) as in the economic sense of our titular noun. In the craft (before art) of painting, *value* or tone, brightness versus darkness, is what dynamizes color within a composition – just as is the case, by analogy (and prototype), with tone and vibrancy and harmony in music. The muted chromatic scaling from "were these" to "worthily" is writing's own gesture or stroke in this graded syllabic vein. And so some more words about "worth" are in order: in banking on the hope of some settlement out of court – or at least sidelining – of a number of recent debates that might otherwise get in the way of the intensive

analysis (not to be hastily mistaken for celebratory and elitist rank-
ing) to come.

Whereas the complexity of Conrad's sentences may seem quintessential in his demanding practice, the phonetic accordion-play
of syllabification in the Hawthorne example is far less likely to be
identified, let alone unmistakably, as Hawthorne's. Such divergent
types of verbal recognition are continually, rather than just alterna-
tively, our subject, since the emphasis on the attentive immersion
to come does not fall primarily on signature styles plural, but on the
singularity of style as a feature common to a vast array of writing
practice. Not *a* style, by contrast with another like or unlike it, but
style in practice across diverse rhetorical habits. Value, too, attaches
to this recognition in a singular way: evaluation as explication, not
in the sense of stratifications or hierarchies. And this is why one
returns again and again to the sentence as the operative unit of style.
Paragraphs, chapter dynamics, mood, attitude, vernacular registers,
rhetorical stance: these and other larger-scale considerations, however vague in certain attributions, render "styles" recognizable in the
loose journalistic sense. Style, singular, is a matter of sentences: their
at once imposed and disclosed form, indeed their verbal matter. Style,
one may say, is the sentencing of idea to diction and its grammar.

VERBAL SURPLUS: ON WHAT TERMS DISCOUNTED?

On a related question of singular versus plural categorizations, I am
preceded by a fellow contributor to this series. And reminded again
that value is not just a starting point, but a potential sticking point as
well. In *The Value of Virginia Woolf*, Madelyn Detloff sets out with
another such (and ultimately related) divide. Her opening sentence:
"One cannot speak of value without implicitly or explicitly speaking
of values"[26] (1). Barbara Herrnstein Smith's *Contingencies of Value* and
John Guillory's *Cultural Capital* organize Detloff's sense of a shifting
spectrum – social, cultural, ethical, political – that would tacitly color
the sheerly relative and often class-based terms, respectively, of what

one *invests in* when reading. So what is the further value of style if more than a register of the distinctions on which cultural *distinction*, in its own singular sense – as against its "lowbrow" alternative – is meant to rest? A kind of answer, as it happens, comes near the end of Detloff's Introduction (and we'll be coming back to this at the end of ours), where she would seem to resist even-handedly not only the reductions of cultural critique in response to "high" art's exclusivity but of cognitive narratology as well, citing Woolf on the nonutility of literary words, their operation apart from referential "use" value. Detloff reflects here on the matter of Woolf's difficult yet productive "virtuosity," insisting that "to pin down the value of Woolf's words – suggesting, for example, that complex fiction such as Woolf's stimulates neurological responses that enhance our capacity for pattern recognition, empathy, or invention – would be to reduce the power of fiction" (12): to trivialize it, that is, as something like an exercise program in imaginative fitness. What, then, is the "power" in question – if not, otherwise, a mere cultural power play? And how can it be given a fit "evaluation" by attention to style?

So Barthes again, and the yields, definitional rather than merely aesthetic, of "slow motion" reading in the "cinematographic sense" of "decomposition" (12). Given his commitment, as spelled out on the first page of *S/Z* under the subtitle "Evaluation," to an unremitting rigor in the analysis of text – a regimen characterized as "subjecting it from the outset to a basic typology, to an evaluation" (3) – the subsequent inquiry and its appositional restatement follow naturally enough: "How then posit the value of a text? How establish a basic typology of texts?" Ask that of sentences in particular, not just of text (the latter Barthes's concern), and we are closer to this book's topic – without having strayed far from the logic of *S/Z*. What "types" of formal pressure, in diction, syntax, figure, rhetoric, are being brought to bear on a selected sentence as an active phrasing rather than just a phrased depiction? What "value" is imparted to meaning *in the process*, with the *in* of that question conveying more than its usual idiomatic sense: namely, what *internally* felt value as process, as activity, as action? This action is what Barthes identifies as "practice." He insists that neither "science" (he means linguistics, first of all) nor "ideology" can set the terms of literary analysis, for the former "does not evaluate" and ideology, ranging anywhere from religious to political, is concerned with the "value of representation, not of production." This is the crucial point of departure: "Our evaluation can be linked only to a practice, and this practice is that of writing" (4). Its teleology (a kind of late-1960s' aesthetic "ideology" in itself, of course) has been acted out, and subsequently played out, in the postmodern "writerly" text, stripped of realist baggage: devoid of plausible characters, dialogue, and the like, buoyed sheerly on the eros of enunciation. But its premise, the value of its "practice," remains rooted in the *written* of the read and the readerly, even in so-called classic texts – again, the lexias. So that when, as with Barthes's object of study in Balzac, what has been produced is itself a representation, a narrative, then the activity in question is, after all, the practice of written representation – leading therefore to questions of the "value" of writing itself as narrative production. Or make that: of style in fiction.

Though his topic is poetry instead, we are on adjacent terrain to that held by Charles Altieri's stress on "valuation" in one's immanent appreciation, or understanding, of verse practice, rather than its relative aesthetic assessment.[27] His earliest example is the wily and lordly "syntax" of Claudius's first speech in *Hamlet*. What an "affective" (12) reaction to its ingenuity amounts to is routed through the reader's "sensibility" – in precisely our measuring what poor Hamlet is up against in this theater of rhetoric. "In short, a concern for valuing is what makes close reading into slow reading" (30). It is as if, like Hamlet, we are given pause. "And it ultimately shows why instrumental reading is so reductive because it locates value only in application rather than in participation" (30). One is inclined here to vary the telling ambivalence of Altieri's own title – in the double sense of *Reckoning with the Imagination*: coming to terms with it while thinking along with, and through, it. On a similar understanding, the slow reading invited by a certain weight of fictional prose requires that – for any engaged sense of storyline and character, let alone for noticing the linguistic intersections that weave them into view – one must reckon with style.

This cross-wiring – this interpenetration – of stylistic effects, of whatever sort, may in itself take us close to a certain redefinition of style: not just as a shaping function, in the patterned recurrences theorized by Jakobson, but as the release of productive verbal interferences: internal shifts in the very force field of linguistic (even before representational) effect. In this light, extravagant grammar can become its own kind of figure: a contoured rhythmic surplus over and above mere depiction, yet a surplus that often seems internalized by the momentum of prose as its own kind of generative semantic structure. The reverse proposal emerges by a further structuring logic, as well. For figures (metaphors, personifications) have their own grammar – their articulated interrelation with the literal. This involves not just the prepositional "like" or the subordinator "as if" in the work of simile, but an underlying grammar internal to analogy's own operation: its own variable axis of comparison, substitution, displacement. In such a deep syntax of correlation, *this* links to – resembles, equals, displaces – *that* only in pointing to unspoken common denominators in triangulation with the manifest alignment of attributes. In other words, figuration can structure the sentence at a level no less deep and rudimentary than syntax. It is not ancillary, still less just decorative in its strongest examples, but *configuring*. The same goes for the relation of diction to syntax, each redefining the structure and function of the other in progress – and thus conflating the Jakobsonian categories of selection and combination at the most rudimentary level of word choice versus word order. It is in this way that the latter can seem to reorder the very logic of selection (*this* word versus its near alternative in *that*) even while rerouted in its own trajectory by the unexpected second meaning of a given **lexeme**. So it goes – all tested at the level of the single sentence – and with one more preliminary example coming, to prime us for the chapters ahead.

Anticipating this further instance from a laconic knot of syntax in the midst of Woolf's modernist stream of consciousness, we can stand back for a moment. Style, one might propose, with Woolf's own stress on inutility in mind (from Detloff's *Value of* study, again), is a name for the functioning of writing before its use function – or in Barthes's terms, a "practice" made available, but not equivalent, to representation. It is the best name for just that quality of writing whose active notice, being essentially literary, can be isolated, if only conceptually, from the other aspects of fiction reading – isolated as that which orchestrates the rest through its shaping force (this sense of its "power"). And style, therefore, one is further tempted to say, is what introduces the very urge for "evaluation" in the encounter with such writing when it is as challenging and gorgeous as it is, for instance, in Woolf's prose: a sorting of value (and phrasal values) – through both slow reading and rereading – that thereby exposes the comparable reductiveness of the quasi-economic paradigm of cultural cachet as well as the raw cognitive model of perceptual calisthenics. Style, engaged by reading, elicits a response that cannot be predominantly hierarchal or even entirely contingent, let alone just an exercise in attention, given its far more immediate hold on us – in the very grip it gives to narrative.

So a single sentence from Woolf, though not deliberated over in the *Value of* volume, can speak volumes in itself. The finality of death is often a test of style in the coming pages, the blankness interfaced by words – even when not wholly faced up to, let alone faced down, by them. Recall, then, a particular achievement of such style, one of the most memorable in modern literature, from Woolf's *To the Lighthouse*. It is a sentence about the grammar of tense itself, one where the temporal logic of repetition has no descriptive use, even as sheer emphasis – except to break, twice over, from the ongoing: that of both the husband's own participial "stumbling" and his wife's life. The sentence in question is one of fiction's incontrovertible show-stoppers: "Mr. Ramsay, stumbling along a passage one dark morning, stretched his arms out, but Mrs. Ramsay having died rather suddenly the night before, his arms, though stretched out, remained empty."[28] Every reader, when caught up in the metaphysical rhythms of the "Time Passes" section of the novel, is blindsided by this passage the first time through. But to be dumbstruck by it is something else. Instead, the effort at an exacting description of the effect *is* evaluation – and vice versa – beginning with one's reaction to the searing existential understatement of "rather suddenly" for the absolute abruptness of any death moment.

But only beginning there. The interrupting participial doublet (present progressive tense choked off in a past perfect: "having died") is obtruded in that grammar of half clause/half phrase known as an **absolute construction** – and perhaps as absolute in tactical deployment here as any in English literature: no "because" or "since" of anticipation, just the thud of mortal cause in the same syntactic breath as bereft effect. (Not at all undeserved, then, for this term to get accidental pride of place in the limited alphabetized inventory that concludes this book, coming before the more prevalent assonance called out from Dickens, above, and separately theorized by Jakobson – as such glossary terms will be bolded for immediate recognition at their first appearance from here out.) In Woolf's passage, this uncannily well-judged syntactic bypass of the main grammatical vector is followed by the prolonged moment of an almost freeze-frame effect in the repeated intransitive verb phrase "stretched out," first in active, then in passive form (implicitly "by him," and with no object of embrace ever again to meet the predication of its reach). **Mimetic syntax** like this, if we notice it as such (at a certain level of abstraction) overstretches its own needs, overreaches here into its own sad vacuum – as only made more obvious by the passage's vexed textual history.[29] And just as this grammar thereby turns figurative in its own right, it reveals the **metaphor** (or barely active **dead metaphor**, more to the point) lurking from the first in "dark": not only literal cause of the husband's stumbling but also emotional effect of his bleak discovery. This effect is what, in turn, so hauntingly displaces "remained empty" from a simple past to a kind of perpetual present of subtracted presence in Mrs. Ramsay's (thus syntactically figured) removal forever from this world.

Whatever "cultural capital" one might think to brandish by appreciating the unique *tense-ion* of this elastic grammatical span and its surprise snap, the value that style contributes – the value that style constitutes – is of a different order, and more specific measure, than some prestige of literary recognition in the precincts of elite reading. Rather, its value is that of language's underlying order. Woolf's rhetorical effect stands. You don't have to be high-toned to appreciate it as "serious literature." You just have to hear its fraught tonalities and its taut predication. The "values" it brings in tow are most importantly a matter of phrasal shading. To any reader with open ears for the pivotal give and backlash of this grammar, Woolf's phrasing offers a kind of parable of syntax per se in its ability to elicit temporal interdependencies – and their sometimes grievous irreversibility. That's what words are worth in any evaluation, any typology, of their convergent effects in action, here across the precipitous twist of this one sentence. Other sentences, hopefully as instructive, and sometimes as mesmerizing, await.

As such further samples of stylistic force and undertow are about to sort themselves into rather arbitrarily partitioned sectors of analysis, this book puts itself forward as a venture in what used to be called "practical criticism" – answering in kind, as it were, to writerly "practice" in Barthes's sense. And it is one particular aspect of that critical practice, long lapsed, that is pointedly being brought back for rethinking in what may seem, so little exercised has it been lately, a virtually experimental (rather than traditional) mode of textual attention. For this reason, in a heuristic more than a combative or turf-clearing spirit, there is much to be gained from defining stylistic reading against what it isn't: not just hermeneutically *close* rather than statistically *far*; neither quantitative nor in some tendentious way qualitative or hierarchical; neither surface-bound nor strictly symptomatic and intertextual – but instead, once again, a *deep* reading, formative rather than formalistic. This is because the depth at issue is that of the linguistic substrate itself from which any verbal patterning emerges, takes form, and asserts itself, or we might say *fields its force* – often with a coordinated teamwork mapped out in forward moves, lateral relays, and unexpected conversions.

In this sense, the *value* of style can either be cashed out in immediate appreciation or reinvested in apprehending the founding energetics, and sometimes the definitive friction, of the genre we call prose fiction – but whose prose is too seldom engaged with in commentary. So to characterize the spotty examples thus far as merely down payments on the wealth of material that will eventually be put into circulation for analysis (and the far greater range of instances implicit) – as funded by language under the sign and gauge of style – is only to bear in mind the more intrinsic economies of phrasing and response we've begun to x-ray in the literary sentence itself. These include the whole shared stratum of affective investment and net return that literary prose can broker, whether in inquisitive lift, recoil, perplexity, or, again, delight.

Even in a book many times this length, illustration would be only woefully partial. Yet the consolation for this is, I trust, the ease of extrapolation from what does follow. Everything to be said and suggested – and everything suggestive in the cited passages themselves – applies more widely. Instances exceed principle a thousand times over. In just this respect, the deep reading of any one passage has a way of tunneling through to others like it, sharing in the same subterranean linguistic pressures – and possibilities – that rise to style. And that await our close concern as such: our valuative notice. So ask it again, differently this time. Not: style as opposed to what? Rather: style as the manifestation of what? What undergirds and structures the shapes of phrase? The fact that there is a new, but not entirely new, answer for each new example takes us back, again and again, from literature to the language it is made of. Yet by the same token, seen and heard from the perspective of that funding source, style is what writing makes of language, evincing the values of its own availability for phrase. A book like this might be thought of as a portfolio of investment strategies in the tendering of attention.

ACCRUING TO WHOM?: A BRIEF USER'S GUIDE

Given the specific procedures of the present volume, however, the question remains: with an extracted value for whom especially? This study (mainly a prompt to more study like it) is intended for two-related audiences – approximating one concerted readership. It is for students of all ages, and any degree of institutional affiliation, who wish to expand their descriptive toolkit in analyzing the writing they care about; it is for aspiring or even accomplished writers eager to attune themselves further to previous achievements in the prose sentence. And where the two audiences converge, this twin readership approaches to a single *writership*. In the book's very format, a sense of its combined target may come through at a glance. For if the bolding of keywords gives this "companion" to memorable sentences the look of a writing handbook or primer – and if incorporating what might have been just an appended glossary as instead a summary phase of the discussion, indeed its capping chapter, seems further to imply an integral application of its terms – this is all true to the pedagogic spirit of the volume. For it is a book that has emerged in part from the teaching of fictional prose to a craft-oriented group of undergraduates in my home department's new creative writing track. Any such classroom venture quickly makes apparent the feedback loop between the appreciative study of literary writing and the exercise of one's own verbal powers – and not just in some eventual transition to creative prose, whether in short stories, memoirs, essayism, or what have you.

Before that – beneath that, foundational – it is the osmosis as well as the lesson of style that feeds more immediately into the prose of one's own careful appreciation. *The Value of Style in Fiction*, though more strictly literary in its focus as a critical manifesto, would thus sit happily, nonetheless, on the same shelf as practical composition manuals that also offer principle by test case, instructing in stylistic technique by decisive example.[30] But the process exercised here involves an extra turn in its less direct circuit of uptake. If, for many readers, the blend of refresher course and new terminological roster in the closing "Inventory" helps not just in spotting (whether or not inclined toward technically naming it) a stylistic device, but also in potentially mobilizing it more knowingly in one's own prose, then that chapter's twin purpose has been served. So the emphasis of these pages is different from simply stressing that we learn by modeling and imitation, learn by doing our version of the same. Rather, we first learn by spelling out to ourselves what strong writing does, can do – or in other words (necessarily other words) by *writing it out*, replaying the pleasure of recognition with descriptive words of our own.

The finding of those words is the very exercise of analytic investment. Once attention is armed with a modicum of linguistic and rhetorical terminology, its own additional words are fetched from a whole spectrum of more or less metaphoric and *ad hoc* approximations for the furnished structure of selected passages. Such is a vocabulary, in my own descriptors, that can be drawn by turns from the sciences of physics or biology (inertial force, engineered form, organic sedimentation, aberrant outcrops), from psychology (unconscious drives and returns of the repressed), from stereo acoustics (multichanneled phonetic effects and their muted reverb), on and on, you name it. Or, more to the point, rename it: putting into new words of your own the already worded – always an exercise in what can only be called *creative rewriting*. It is a kind of translation, but from the inside out. Writing about writing in Dickens or Woolf, Melville or Faulkner, is most open to discovery when it is least stinting in the imaginative flexion of its own prose. Appreciation of this sort doesn't set out to reproduce the style under analysis, but only to replicate (by way of honoring) its complexities, or its pressurized simplicities, in a diction and cadence of one's own.

Perception begins, of course, in really reading along. And the subsequent interpretive effort isn't ultimately to catch the splendor or surprise of a given sentence in a digested nugget of response, but more intimately to *write along* with it, a second time through, in the meshed dynamics of analysis.[31] If I were proposing this mainly to defend against potential charges, regarding occasional discussions ahead, of a rather dense flux of intuition in my own unfolding account of selected linguistic intricacies, that would be justification enough. For this book practices not so much what it preaches as what it invites – in attending without letup to even the most strenuous effects for which fictional prose can reach. And by which it can thus reach us. Not just witnessing to the invested pleasure of a truly *literary* criticism, such attention becomes a committed and unrelenting apprenticeship in style's own challenges.

2 Emergent Turns
Defoe toward Dickens

So we begin, not with signature stylistic features from author to author, but with a few signal moments of more broadly categorized effect. As signposts in the signifying options available to, and varied by, a self-consciously unfolding lineage of the novel form, these isolated moments are to be estimated in their distinct local force – rather than comparatively esteemed. To this end, the test of value rather than quality – a valuation phrasal and rhetorical – requires checks and counterexamples, filling in the gaps between lauded masters of verbal finesse with other and still major writing that may seem less immediately "stylish." Deep down, there is in fact nothing "ish" about our topic in the ordinary sense of that suffix, nor necessarily mannered or "stylized" about its evidence. Rather, style is the *manner of writing* in whatever period or key. Style inheres, rather than adheres.

We are therefore concerned not with something "styled" after the fact, inflected over and above meaning, but with the style of meaning in its own right, the *form* it takes – or, better yet, conferring no priority, the expressive gestures that *form* it. Since stylistic attention does not single out stylish writing, whatever that might be, it follows that prose style, as investigated here, is, in the truest literary sense, a quotient of all narrative fiction. This is because the affiliation between narrative meaning and narrative wording, story and style, is no less intrinsic to prose that deliberately sounds unworked and spontaneous than it is to the most magisterially controlled pacing or the most overwrought frenzy of grammar, diction, or image. And this, in turn, is because style, deep down again, is the very manifestation of the medium in its tapped possibilities.

Deep down – but how deep? And, more specifically, where? Only the byplay between contrastive examples is likely to suspend attention to surface contours – even while noting and probing them – long enough to reveal their conditioning linguistic base. That is the premise here. Writing about the "value" of style – or say "values," plural, but not in the sense of ethical inferences, but rather of tonal valences – requires a move beyond all local rankings or preferences. This doesn't come naturally. In critical writing, one often plays favorites. In this sense, a leading difficulty of a book like this – a consideration necessarily ranging over different centuries, modes, and verbal proclivities – offers, in just the challenge posed by such variety, an undeniable heuristic potential. The problem is *leading* in the happier sense as well, pointing beyond habits of taste to factors of its instigation. Stylistic attention amounts in this way to a sharpening of focus in a fuller depth of field. Rather than sorting in search of high points within a received (or even private) pantheon, the effort is to highlight effects operating along a broad spectrum of verbal diversity. Which sends us back to early efforts in the genre's fledging gestures of self-expression, in all of the capacities and aptitudes of English phrasing first experimented with in such eighteenth-century fiction – notably in its varieties of allegiance to linguistic traditions derived from either Latinate or Anglo-Saxon word streams. So the historical question takes shape: what news about the emergent genre of prose fiction was delivered by wording alone, over against its unprecedented range of content? Or ask it from another angle: how prose-dependent were the new narrative patterns opened up by a fictional storytelling that pushed beyond romance and allegory on the long road to, and later well beyond, realism?

The very question of style is in this sense a genre consideration. And genre is, first of all, a decidedly historical phenomenon. For our purposes, in revisiting the initial century of traffic along the increasingly crowded route toward Victorian realism, such genre-founding authors of the eighteenth century as Daniel Defoe, Henry Fielding, and Laurence Sterne, as well as the writers following in their immediate path, invite comparative analysis rather than a search for superlative instances among treasured pet sentences. Through it all, however, the sentence remains the unit of measure. Period idiom and its wit, syntactic expectations, rhetorical leeway, figurative scope, the gist of visual imagery: all differ productively from writer to writer – and produce differences that, however muted in one novel or another, or boosted, constitute any given sentence's stylistic register. For exemplification, there's no reason to cast about in search of *more* style rather than less; attention is aimed at how a palpable diversity of effects, some seemingly straightforward and colorless, may tell us more about style *per se* – in the process of their own storytelling – than one would learn merely from consulting certain showstopping passages in the annals of canonical flamboyance.

We begin, then, with prose where one can spot certain rules and opportunities being instituted in process, rather than merely burnished or veered from. Style is undeniably a test of the genre possibilities it manifests. But one needs to go further – or farther back – or, say again, deeper. Not just facilitated, the novel as genre is *founded* by, and on, just this stylistic testing: a *finding of its way* in words. These are words low-keyed at first in Defoe, later prolix and satiric in Fielding, later yet fervid and extravagant in Sterne, then again coolly ironic in a more neoclassical vein by the time of Austen. Like the genre itself, and the rhythms of its representational aesthetic, we can start slow – even as we soon race quickly ahead.

But we can best start from theory as well as instance – as part of the topographic map to be followed out. As taken up in the Introduction – and here paraphrasing only slightly, leaving behind his Russian formalist terminology – David Bordwell demonstrates how the act of narration is the process by which *structure* (the sequence of presentation) "plus style" cooperate in "cueing and channeling" the reader's *construction*, rather than just recognition, of the story. This isn't putting the cart before the horse, just the discourse before the story, the latter materialized only through the former. Reading (or in Bordwell's screen territory, viewing) builds what it apprehends, orders the articulation of any given plot from the signals conveyed in part by "style." This cognitive logic translates from screen to page just fine, once all the necessary adjustments in the calibration of lexigraphic rather than cinematographic descriptions are in place. But at the sentence level, emphasis shifts. In individual syntactic sequences, style alone, not ancillary but constitutive, guides the reader's verbal response. Or say, instead: style formulates the **microplot** of a given sentence, an infrastructure of event that one might call the *stylistic moment*. It is thus style, sentence by sentence, that renders the story we're reading at least subtly different from any that might be otherwise phrased around the same raw ingredients. Or, more to the point yet, style in prose fiction makes the local depiction, the narrative action, not just other than it might have been, but *makes* it, renders it: constructs it from the ground up, configures it in the mind of reading. And this involves a sense, as proposed in the Introduction, that grammar can be as figurative as any rhetorical **trope** (etymologically, a "turning aside"), with an inverted or suspended syntax, for instance, as quick to match depiction in particular cases – as readily "thematized" – as any simile or metaphor.

Consider in this light a single sentence out of later Dickens – from the fully achieved moment of Victorian fiction – that in fact comes close, as his phrasings often do, to cinematic prototypes and paradigms: here a scene of spectatorship itself in the familiar mise-en-scène of a crowded courtroom drama. In Charles Darnay's final trial in *A Tale of Two Cities* (1859), the famous "cinematic" aspects of Dickensian "montage" are tangibly syntactic. In setting the stage for the sealed doom of Darnay in the coming chapter's cited document, this single, breathlessly levitated **periodic** sentence, on the brink of that incriminating found manuscript in full enunciation, isn't so much a cliff-hanger as a pressurized narrative hiatus waiting to explode:

In a dead silence and stillness – the prisoner under trial looking lovingly at his wife, his wife only looking from him to look with solicitude at her father, Doctor Manette keeping his eyes fixed on the reader, Madame Defarge never taking hers from the prisoner, Defarge never taking his from his feasting wife, and all the other eyes there intent upon the Doctor, who saw none of them – the paper was read, as follows.

Barreling down on the **passive** grammar of the kernel clause postponed until syntactic closure, and absent any specified agent of an action identified as doing the reading, the sentence enacts its own anxiety – while anticipating the worst in that idiomatic dead metaphor of "dead silence" in a zombie-like reactivation. Half a dozen absolute constructions (that first inventory item again, as noted previously, along with dead metaphor, in Woolf) – pitched between clause and phrase in a subject–verb linkage without a **finite** grammar of tense, all compacted and simultaneous – serve to cross-map the sight lines of anticipation in a present progressive tense of tension itself. In a paradoxical state of hyperkinetic stalling at the plot level, of suspense rendered by grammar itself, the sentence form powers ahead, *drawing on* its established patterns in both senses: drawing them further *out* in recursive returns while drawing syntax *forward* to new facets of the described event: the event of pregnant pause itself.

Astonishing. But, let's face it, Dickens is too easy, his prose facility too ready – and inexhaustible – an examplar. His acrobatic style could illustrate almost anything and everything in the panoply of stylistic energy, ingenuity, and extravagance. And not least the optical grammar of cinema in anticipation. So, before looking back to genre origins, let's content ourselves with only one more example to this effect, famous – from his last completed novel. A giant mirror over the *nouveau riche* dinner table in the second chapter of *Our Mutual Friend* is fragmented in the very grammar of its own intact beholding. Or see it, look into it, this way: as the sheer impersonal surface of narrative focus all told in this episode of piecemeal omniscience. In association with its varnished more than polished owners, the so-called Veneerings, their showcase mirror serves to isolate one depthless character after another for an ironic ethical, as well as optical, inspection: "The great looking-glass above the sideboard, reflects the table and the company," with that unwarranted comma marking a latent and available pause for insertion of the nine unmoored present-tense verb **fragments** to follow: "Reflects the new Veneering crest ... Reflects Veneering ... Reflects Mrs. Veneering ... Reflects Podsnap; prosperously feeding," on and on – as if always further in to this unreal recessional space. It isn't that the mirror has been shattered in its luxuriant complacency by the ill-sorted cross section of society it duplicates. Rather, the more tangibly precinematic effect at work, amid the powerfully optical deconstruction of the mere *look of society*, derives from the fact that the assembly exists for the moment only in this showy plane of material display. Dickens's verbal gauge of superficiality is unforgettable. Yet *The Value of Style in Fiction* is not, I stress again, about what there is to say concerning such incomparable authorship, in the case either of Dickens or of other acknowledged verbal innovators. Instead, it concerns what writing *has to say for itself* in the reading of any major – or minor – author. So, as anticipated, we can best move forward at first by stepping back. Whatever else Dickens was, he wasn't without predecessors.

A FIRST CENTURY IN FAST-FORWARD, 1719–1819

Encountering someone else's "story" – *story* in either sense, told of or by – is the primal desire of the novel reader. Style is its medium: language *in situ*, linguistic possibility localized. Whereas, midway through the novel's second century, a low-keyed **double entendre** at the start of Dickens's *David Copperfield* (1850) – for "life" as both human duration and its "life story" alike, biology and fictional biography – gets Dickens's narrator going, the genre's earlier determination, in works like those of Daniel Defoe, would have been more likely to announce itself this way: "To begin my life with the beginning of my life, I was born to record." To document, to transcribe: not to invent. So in outfitting any book's attempt at a broad-based critical laboratory devoted to style's variety and mutations over literary-historical time, one needs to return first to the genre's incubation ward. One goes there not in search of an origin story but for a sense of the story forms gestated in the novel's inaugural century – not just midwifed – in good part by style. Doing so doesn't offer some prelude to richer stylistic analysis. It is the thing itself. For the novel came to be in the womb of prose's shaping possibilities – and grew to maturity through the choices made for it by an escalating mix of cultural expectation and verbal dexterity. Well before the established poetic license of a first-person *bildungsroman* like *David Copperfield*, the genre-founding documentation of *Robinson Crusoe*, whose title page

announces "Written by Himself," is obliged to introduce its eponymous hero, as retrospective narrator, in the generational grammar of
a plausible family lineage. Style sets the tone by the subtraction of all
rhetorical décor. To put it differently, style orients even as it articulates. It is both determining frame and incidental feature.

So we look now to polar extremes in the novel's first century:
the pseudo-documentary realism of *Robinson Crusoe* (1719) versus the
rhetorical lather of Laurence Sterne's *A Sentimental Journey through
France and Italy* (1768). In Defoe, scrupulous fidelity of detail will in
the long run, after shipwreck and eventual bonding with Friday, evolve
into measured affect and reciprocated human feeling. In Sterne, quite
the reverse trajectory is laid out. A hypertrophic sensitivity on the narrator Yorick's part – including his overreaction, at one turning point,
to the conjured (rather than encountered) grief of others – redounds
there, midway in the narrator's sentimental itinerary, to the emotional tenor of melodramatic narration *per se* (unabashedly fictional,
at that): an inset and withering episode of strictly imaginary prison
grief. As would have been unthinkable in the more carefully policed
veridicality of *Crusoe*, authenticity of report lapses, in Yorick's convulsive reverie, into pure projection: a motivated aesthetic of frantically
lamented deprivation at one (entirely invented) remove. This draining
thought experiment in fellow-feeling transpires most obviously in
the prose – the style – of the exclamatory, emotionally indulgent, and
sporadically unhinged narrator, and does so as the constitutive effect
of the new subgenre, the sentimental novel, in which he finds himself.

Our beginning with an earlier, and foundational, novel by Defoe,
before considering its temperamental – and rhetorical – antithesis
in Sterne, also serves the purpose here, in a book on the prose of
prose fiction, of confirming a sense that there is no such thing as
"no style" in a fictional paragraph. There are only degrees of invention and intensity marked as such, as much in the mode of minus as
of overplus. But marked, nonetheless – not stylistically negligible.
In *Crusoe*, action is prepared long in advance of any real adventure
by a stylistically abetted (because clinically bland and overexplicit)
gesture of what we might call authorial authentication. It is the
style of the flatly unstylish itself. The imaginary is realized, indeed

valorized, only insofar as it is backed by facts, whereas in the throes of Sterne's sentimentality, as we are to see by contrast, the real stuff of fiction is verified only in so far as it is imaginable by the sensitized mind. In each case, as it happens, the simplest linking words of placement and interrelation, the **prepositions**, serve to chart either the patient inertness or the fervor, respectively, of these contrastive procedures. If, as proposed just now, style is frame as well as feature, then the larger frame – or, say, the underlying parameter – of style is inevitably language itself. The smallest parts of speech, prepositions, adverbs, articles, along with the grammatical ballast of nouns and verbs, all play their part. And what they perform is our topic: a case of prose as particulate matter under dramatic motivation.

At the opening of *Crusoe*, prepositions are initially divided between routine idioms of time and place before bearing down on nested generational testimony, the whole effect almost legalistically neutral in its dutiful lumpiness: "I was born *in* the year 1632, *in* the city of York, *of* a good family, though not *of* that country, my father being a foreigner *of* Bremen, who settled first *at* Hull"[1] – a quadruple shunting from family through city to country of origin and back to locus of immigration. All this is so much a spatialization of human relations and their genealogy that, in what follows, the fussy formality of "from whence" and "from whom," as adverbial doublets, falls right into line with it – in a slack build toward a suddenly assertive shift from passive to reflexive grammar. This takes place, and takes syntactical time, in a phrasing that, extricating itself from an initially terraced bank of subordination, rounds out one long sentence in making a single preliminary and establishing point about the hero's patrilineage and its grafted family tree (prepositions again pointing the way). For Crusoe's father "got a good estate *by* merchandise, and leaving *off* his trade, lived afterwards *at* York, *from whence* he had married my mother, whose relations were named Robinson, a very good family in that country, and *from whom* I was called Robinson Kreutznaer" (7). It is as the narrating hero is christened not *by* his mother, who disappears as agent into her own family name (the very name as if personified as "whom"), but "from" her – as the mere channeling of a lineage. A semicolon then sets this off from the upshot that the book's title needs by way of explication, turning as it does on the equally clipped but more discursive prepositional "by" (i.e., *through the intervening function of*): "but, *by* the usual corruption of words in England, we are now called – nay we call ourselves and write our name – Crusoe" (7).

"Called" by others is one thing, but performing that nomination for oneself, even as a collective family act, constitutes an owning *to* one's genealogy and its eroded etymology at once, however linguistically adulterated it has become over habitual time. Personal history here is entirely an act of wording – and even, in the avowed case before us, of writing. Received identification is matched by a self-asserted claim on it when taking up the pen. So potent is this switch between passive and active nomination in the launching of a written fiction that it seems the model, a century and a half in advance, for the similar (if reversed) grammatical play between self-naming and the same moniker's wider currency in Dickens's *Great Expectations*. For there we find a preliterate Pip lisping by elision each inherited disyllable of his father's name in opening his own autobiographical document with an etymological backstory even briefer than that of the corrupted "Crusoe": "My father's family name being Pirrip, and my Christian name Philip, my infant tongue could make of both names nothing longer or more explicit than Pip. So, I called myself Pip, and came to be called Pip."[2] It is just this laying claim to a truncated name – if already *self*-compressed in Pip's case – that finds its canonical precedent in the degenerated name, Crusoe, that, following the family commitment, he does more than just call himself, he inscribes himself – and before our very eyes in the adventures attached to his name. Again: not just "answer to," as it were, but the double acknowledgment that "we call ourselves" and even "write our name – Crusoe." Given that all articulation in the pages of the novel to come, nomenclature not least, is fictive script, a reader of Defoe – at least second time through – can be forgiven for hearing the name steeped as well, in this touchstone case, by undertones of all the ill-fated high-seas *cruising* so definitively to come. *Nomen est omen*, in the form of a faint **punning** undertone, for this man who would write not just his family prehistory but his recently elapsed adventure.

Nothing could sound less documentary than the antithetical effusions of Laurence Sterne, reminding us that irony, however elusive, is one clear barometer of style. Irony: saying one thing while meaning another. The touchstone of discrepancy in such cases is essentially linguistic. Irony's opposite, in a forced and studied sincerity, is often harder to parse in stylistic terms. Yet, in some cases, the heartfelt tests itself against the phrasal templates of cliché, allusion, and the vitality of grammar *per se* – as if to interrogate, indeed to ironize, its own limits. In Sterne's quintessential fiction of the eighteenth-century cult of sensibility, the short chapter "The Captive, Paris," shows the narrator, Yorick, grown captive to his own sympathetic reverie. Having mused out loud on how prison, the Bastille in particular, isn't necessarily so bad for many people, free room and board at least, he then, in a self-chastising manner, tries thinking better of this consolatory view. But the canvas is too large at first for concentration and its intended ethical concern. In a passage that can't help but trivialize, from the start, the froth of empathy self-generated by Yorick, the very pose of his contemplation is itself routine: "I sat down close to my table, and leaning my head upon my hand, I began to figure to myself the miseries of confinement. I was in a right frame for it, and so I gave full scope to my imagination."[3] Good for you. The obvious "frame" is pictorial, with pensiveness frozen in its most cliché pose. But "scope," however well intentioned, isn't focus: "I was going to begin with the millions of my fellow-creatures born to no inheritance but slavery: but finding, however affecting the picture was, that I could not bring it near me" (201) – could not, to press on the spatial metaphor as in fact a somatic one, make it *touching* enough. Given that "the multitude of sad groups in it did but distract me – ," he realizes, after that default punctuation (a typographic dash immediately repeated at the start of the next paragraph, as he catches his breath again), that another tack was necessary. Not being able to "bring it near me" says it all: a sympathy that must, even in its most rudimentary ethics, be made proximate, personal – or the next best thing, as we are now to see: in effect, *novelized*.

Yes, a fiction must be inserted, however awkwardly. "I took a single captive …," where that "took," with its momentary flare-up of idiomatic ambiguity, evokes a prephotographic sense of "taking a likeness" in the mind's eye – even as it deflects the aggressive sense of "taking captive" it is meant to lament. I imagined what jail would really be like: that's, of course, the sense. But the very act of attention, fabricated with this imaginary victim, becomes an act of lockdown and solitary confinement, for "having first shut him up in his dungeon, I then look'd through the twilight of his grated door to take his picture" (201). Giving flesh to the abstract idea of imprisoned energies, this indulgent version of embodiment (a virtual parody of Boxall's emphasis in *The Value of the Novel*), for all its self-absorbed best of intentions, perpetrates a further dehumanization. The passage continues: "I beheld his body half-wasted away with long expectation and confinement, and felt what kind of sickness of the heart it was which arises from hope deferr'd" (202). The straightforward Biblical proverb, "hope deferred makes the heart sick," is swollen into delayed recognition in the strained **circumlocution** "what kind of ... it was which." By an almost mimetic logic of syntax, wordiness seems taking the time necessary for the formulaic to sink in as felt. But as sympathy mounts to a self-stoked boil, the **paratactic** grammar of dashes (the punctuation true to its name) offers what amounts to horizontal exclamation marks on the breathless run. For, according to the exact iambic clocking in of this duration (an effect Sterne wills to Dickens) "*in* thirty years the western breeze had not once fann'd his blood." And "he had seen no sun, no moon, all that time, nor ...," where those last enchained negatives seem phonetically clutching at the very enunciation of withdrawn diurnal manifestations (see*n* *no* su*n*, *no* moo*n* *nor* ...), as if obliterating them further. "[N]or," worse yet, as the sentence plunges headlong toward a paragraph break, "had the voice of friend or kinsman breathed through his lattice. – His children – " (202). It is an arresting specter of isolation that precipitates the next paragraph of defensively shifted focus: "But here my heart began to bleed – and I was forced to go on with another part of the portrait."

After that pivotal cliché "began to bleed," the imagined prisoner has become so real, in this conjectural portrayal, this conjuration, that he himself looks out upon his sympathizer – from beneath the prepositional weight of his stylistically evoked abjection – across a further paratactic chain busy with the victim's misery.

We continue, that is, to "valuate" (Altieri) – within a general tendency of sentimental rhetoric – not just the style of Sterne's fiction, but the style of a willful fiction within it, heavy with the incarcerated sufferer's pre-posited (prepositional) fate: "He was sitting *upon* the ground *upon* a little straw, in the furthest corner of his dungeon, which was alternately his chair and bed" (202). Such is the dead weight of his abjection, made perverse when he notices he is being surveilled by sympathy itself. Here, then, is an unnerving version of **metalepsis**: the "author" made privy to the very character he invents, who responds opaquely to this sensed but disembodied prying eye in a further cross-vectoring of prepositions: "As I darkened the little light he had, he lifted *up* a hopeless eye towards the door, then cast it *down*, – shook his head, and went *on* with his work of affliction. I heard his chains *upon* his legs, as he turned his body to lay his little stick *upon* the bundle. – He gave a deep sigh." Four *upon*s structure the passage in a weighted pressure of the material body and of moral imposition at once. It is at this point that the manacled condition has been fully internalized by the ironed prisoner as well as the nonironic conjurer of his illustrative fate, pivoted next around the echo of a second contrastive prepositional pair: "I saw the iron enter *into* his soul! – I burst *into* tears. – I could not sustain the picture of confinement which my fancy had drawn" (203). The bidirectional sharing of pain is not an ethical triumph, but an emotional impasse, the splurt of tears answering to the rush of heart's blood earlier. But no matter how ludicrous this extrusion of feeling, this transport of sentimentality, the "fancy" has been "drawn" before us: the work of fictional exemplum achieved. And sillier excesses of phrasing yet, as we'll see in Fielding, can negotiate comparable investments in the novelistic work of plot.

TONAL TRANSFORMATION: "A CERTAIN DROLLERY IN STILE"

Approximately halfway – in literary historical time and tone – between the stringent deadpan picaresque of adventures mainly confined to

an island, in *Crusoe*, and the roving hypersensitivities of a sentimental grand tour, a purer form of the landlocked picaresque than
Sterne's occurs in Fielding's *Joseph Andrews* (1842). This is a novel
that precedes the introduction of its hero with an entire discourse on
genre, laying special stress on the license of "stile" within the established parameters of narrative form. Fielding's book is proffered as a
comedy, not a parody, shaped by established patterns of resolution,
despite the sometimes farcical nature of its diction. Compared to the
unleashing of "stile" as first-person excess and eccentricity in Sterne,
protocols seem still up for measured debate in Fielding's attempt to
define his chosen mode of prose fiction as, famously, a "comic epic
poem in prose."[4] In all this, he claims, mere farce has been marginal-
ized: "I have hinted this little concerning burlesque, because I have
often heard that name given to performances which have been truly
of the comic kind, from the author's having sometimes admitted it
in his diction only." The point is not to judge a fiction by its diction.
Across a **chiasm**-like ratio and proportion in grammar, advanced
in the following as a taut syntactic analogy, and broaching even its
own **homophonic** lexical play in the bridge between words, the work
of internal echo – and even a hint of **cross-word play** (its elements
however muted and removed from each other) – cements the point,
"for a certain *droll*ery in stile, where characters and sentiments are
perfectly natural, no more constitutes the burlesque, than an empty
pomp and dignity of words, where everything else is mean an*d low*,
can entitle any performance to the appellation of the true sublime."
The syllabic flip of "oll" against "low" is the very point on which the
assertion pivots.

The reader of Fielding's satire need not wait long for examples
of such drollery. With Fielding parodying the self-righteous fetish
made of chastity in Samuel Richardson's novel *Pamela* (1740), he
has his heartthrob hero Joseph, Pamela Andrews's equally chaste and
lethally dashing brother, kept on guard to preserve his own virginity –
and never prematurely to "part with my virtue" (37). All ejacula-
tions are those of his both high- and low-born temptresses. For the
result of his considered and dispassionate restraint is that both the
proud Lady Booby and her servant Mrs. Slipslop, each enamored and

inflamed, are loquaciously maddened by his seeming indifference to their separate blandishments. Both mistress and maid become ladies-in-waiting on the lad's checked temptation. Mrs. Slipslop's lust is the funniest, flabbergasting her own language even more than usual with a dense burst of **malapropism**. Certainly in matters of quoted diction here, burlesque reigns supreme, and the "hard words" with which Joseph is besieged – "hard" in the second sense, difficult as well as harsh – include, by a phonetic grasping at straws, the goofy "sophisticates" (25) for "suffices." Outrage has its own anti-style, we might say, high-toned in its low drollery. But by any grammatical standards, her burlesque rant is more like an anti-style: "If we like a man, the lightest hint sophisticates," with "oppression" a next telling slip for the "impression" she is failing to make on the virgin youth. Finally, in the cascade of sloppy slips, we are treated to the antonym "resulted" for an affection contemptuously unrequited ("insulted"). In linguistic terms, Slipslop chooses at random from the paradigm of past **participles** and inapt **gerund** forms: "Barbarous monster! how have I deserved that my passion should be resulted and treated with ironing?" (26). The term "linguistic barbarism" comes to mind.

Anti-style: because none of this is intended on the character's part. But how does the narrator sound when, rather than in high dudgeon on behalf of his female characters, he has gone into overdrive in his own figurative ingenuity? Such grandstand rhetoric is the real test of genre in the play between comedy and farce – even though hyperbole, parody, and travesty can each serve the purpose in varying degrees on both sides of this permeable dividing line between the funny and the forced. Fielding's style, with its categorical precision and grammatical symmetries, operates, one might say, so that, no matter how overblown in its sarcastic effects, each "single hint sophisticates" by its own cool complexity and nuance.

Examples continue apace. No sooner has Slipslop vented in regard to her unachieved relief than we enter upon an inverted analogy, or "**simile**," as Fielding would call such correlations ("if it were our business to make similes," 37). In later terms for metaphorical analysis in the work of modern rhetoric, the "vehicle" that carries the comparison in this case is so much ahead of the "tenor" of desire it figures that all motive seems subsumed under an indiscriminate and unsaid matrix of *animal passion*. No risk of confusion is attendant on "mixing metaphors" here. We know what, and who, is meant in the coming pocket of rhetoric even before her name is said. Moreover, a later passage shines a curious light back on the demeaning jam-up of metaphors for Slipslop's craving. After a subsequent grab bag of analogies for the contradictory reactions of spurned desire in the case of Lady Booby, the narrator pulls up short: "If it was our present business only to make similes, we could produce many more to this purpose; but a simile (as well as a word) to the wise. – " (37). One such "as in the case of" will always do the job, but a busier pile-on of analogies can be recruited to turn a further trick. So back to Joseph's first trial by fire, where the long-haired lad of "*wanton* ringlets" (31) proves that he has not otherwise earned that **epithet**. Slipslop has just made her rebuffed move, and semicolons are assigned to prosecute the figuration. The resulting sentence, with its globe-trotting range of mammalian and piscatory predation, is, as an elucidation of her motives, absurdity itself:

As when a hungry tigress, who long has traversed the woods in fruitless search, sees within the reach of her claws a lamb, she prepares to leap on her prey; or as a voracious pike, of immense size, surveys through the liquid element a roach or gudgeon, which cannot escape her jaws, opens them wide to swallow the little fish; so did Mrs. Slipslop prepare to lay her violent amorous hands on the poor Joseph (26).

The stylistic burden of this sentence is to hold both similes, both analogies, together in the same mental breath, even while undermining the transparency of each with unexpected skids and backflips of association.

   These invite examination. Technically, the paragraph thus begun has no hint of antecedence for this comparison except the feminine noun, "tigress," that propels it – aiming it back toward Slipslop eventually. And after the gulping sound of "hungry tigress," one suspects that a tacit dead metaphor in the familiar idiom "poor lamb" (for innocent youth) has anticipated the tenor of this figurative vehicle. So, too, does "violent amorous hands" sound two notes at once. Not punctuating the two epithets in a "restrictive" fashion, with each in separate relation to the prehensile body, the rush of modification works to fuse predation and sex – in a mode of congested modification (the **adjective chain**) later perfected by Dickens and willed to modern writing. This work has already been accomplished, of course, without identifying it yet, by the pre-pictured snapshots of nature red in tooth and "claws." And we're only half there. The feral leap upon an unsuspecting body is followed, in a far homelier comedown, by the clash of diction (**Latinate** versus Anglo-Saxon) in "voracious pike," whose threat this time lies in her "jaws" rather than "claws," with grabbing followed by gorging.

And yet, through it all, the hodgepodge of associations in this compounded "simile" has a kind of dialectic twist built into its hyperbole, with the potential release of an underlying third term beyond the simple character of the unsated servant. Two wrongs don't make a right, nor do two discrepant analogues naturally right themselves, unless a third term emerges. As it may here – and beyond the underlying cliché of animal desire. Two different images, a tigress on the prowl, a pike on the troll, offer similes indistinguishable at the level of convergent figuration. It is an effect Dickens will make even more unmistakable in the closer quarters of his vise-like analogies for a prison cell, its dead space then dimly personified as a sentience under negation: "Like a well, like a vault, like a tomb, the prison had no knowledge of the brightness outside."[5] In Fielding's case, however, there is something further, and third, that goes unspoken. The twinned female violence of pouncing on and taking into herself – the danger of clutch and maw, respectively – may well seem to displace and condense the entire nature of the *vagina dentata* phobia that is wryly conjured before Mrs. Slipslop even returns into the story to take her frustrated place in the syntax of this analogy.

We can stand back now. If simile is Fielding's loose name for mere analogy, for any "just as" comparison, then we might adapt it as well, by expansion, for those over-same iterations at the level of sound rather than (or in absorption by) sense: all those rolling droll iterations of vowels and consonants that turn the superficial ripples of assonance and **alliteration** to something more integral, or at least ingrained, than merely decorative. Such obtruded if tuneless music of the letter becomes a quotient or exponent of content, a further power, an inbuilt amplitude. It is in this way that, at an exemplary minimum, a "hungry tigress" keeps casual phrasal company with the hard and soft g's, and chiming *ch*, of "roa*ch* or gu*dg*eon" – and does so through the "liquid element" not only of underwater scavenging, as described, but of silent phonation. For such is an "element," or medium, involving the voice-based choice of a diction by turns burlesque, grotesque, eloquent, and deadpan – but always a matter of passive elocution, of latent vocality, however muted or neutral.

In the foregoing effort to look back briefly at the wide array of verbal effects, and affect, in certain founding gestures of the novel form, three writers is hardly a crowd – though they were scarcely alone, with more and more experimenters all the time finding separate voice, which is to say variant idioms, in the new narrative mode. Defoe's authenticating matter-of-factness, Fielding's hyperbolic sarcasm, Sterne's sentimental urgencies: all flagged by decisions of syntax and vocabulary. As prose fiction propagated and bloomed, tone was crucial. Language was its medium. Style made the difference – and differences – in the sound of its genre: marked by soundings both inward and out, from plumbed ethical inferences to trumpet blasts of invention. Diction and grammar, and their collaboration in figure, were both vigilant and strict in sentencing prose to its chosen forms. As we leave the eighteenth century behind in our cursory sampling – on the way to the next century's full-blown adventures of prose fiction as an established and well-seasoned literary form – what discussion has touched on so far is more than a staggered trio of landmarks. It is also a scan of their tendencies across the more extensive ground of prose narrative. We have, to this point, watched the novel find its footing, in stylistic terms, across a fairly full gamut of rhetorical options and their phrasal permutations. These gestures and adjustments are scarcely just subsyllabic, as most recently in the g-jam of Fielding's burlesque; they are also structural in more encompassing (or undergirding) terms. These conditioning features of narrative have been apparent most clearly in, and within, the fondness for perspectival or documentary reframing in the tonalities, however lightly satiric, of advertised editorial neutrality. Crusoe keeps and shares a journal along with a painstaking memoir; Richardson's characters, as travestied by Fielding, are known to us only through their collected letters; Fielding's satire is promoted as an "authentic history"; Sterne's Yorick comes to us by way of a reconstructed diary or travelogue, its shift of scenes recorded in transit. Prose "fiction" finds its legs by not standing too conspicuously upon them at first. And by the time of Scott, on the eve of Victorian narrative, the habit of deferred authority is so familiar in its genial facetiousness that it can be played to the hilt alongside Austen's unapologetic stories woven out of whole cloth, unattributed in their claim on attention.

But even in Scott, if rarely in Austen, the subsyllabic effects remain, enhanced and ramified, along with other unmistakable texturings of discourse inherited from earlier experimentation. Much depends in the constitution of the novel, that is, on a new *style* of writing in all its varied forms, lexical, grammatical, and figural, with the vocabulary of narration ranging from formal to colloquial, its wording Latinate or native, ornate or monosyllabic, stuffy or sparse. Looking simply at what we have to go on so far, we see how such diction is marshaled at times by the syntax of dry, meticulous subordinations (Defoe), restless paratactic momentum (Sterne), or brandished symmetries of satiric analogy (Fielding). These, among many other structural formations, are routed to a reader's notice by everything from the orientating work of the simplest prepositions to the overstrained "as" of simile. Facilitated thereby are now a practical objectivity, now the febrile flights of empathetic fancy, now the more immediate turmoil of frustrated erotic palpitation. In this, that, and the other manner, the whole scope of stylistic inflection is guided in various ways and shapes by the work of exacting prepositional subordination, the vicissitudes of idiom, the shifting gears of syntax, the contradictions of similitude, and the often tangible phonetic outcropping of syllabic dissonance or (to give it via assonance) extruded euphony, however forced the latter may seem. Just three novels sampled – and all this stylistic evidence on offer: its impact already too unwieldy to categorize in any neat fashion. In the deployments of a given sentence, that is, any number of effects overlap, embed, upend, and transfuse each other at various scales of organization and grip. Style, we see again, is the event of meaning in generation. Strip away the authorial names from this time-lapse genealogy of fiction, and a rough-hewn taxonomy of effects begins to take shape, unruly but useful. A typology – or in Barthes's sense again, an "evaluation." In the process, our inventory of devices keeps growing.

FURTHER SOUNDINGS, 1819–1919

A hundred years after Defoe's benchmark stress in the authenticating pretext of invented story, Sir Walter Scott is found going strong in the same inherited vein with *The Bride of Lammermoor* (1819), at that "centenary" turn of metadocumentary prose fiction, as well as a year later in *Ivanhoe* (1920). As Scott graduates from popular poetry to best-selling historical novels, his prose remains a product, in part, of Romantic verse habits and their cult of sonority as a kind of displaced natural song – all that lilting timbre of skylarks, nightingales, west winds, and the like in the great lyrics. Evidently enough, Scott's own regional verse narratives are inflected by the trend as well, even though subsumed to his heavier reliance on end rhyme. In their prose equivalents, the habit of editorial frames remains, enclosing the logic of any such sound play in the premise of found manuscript or pretended historical compilation. A century of experimentation in the novel form has not exhausted the rhetorical fun of documentary truth-claims or edited papers (with Dickens's *Pickwick Papers* waiting in the wings, two decades away, to prove it). Nor would readers have been surprised to see the format revived a century later yet, as we'll note at the close of this chapter, in Joseph Conrad's 1919 *Arrow of Gold*. Audiences continue playing the game, or letting it be played on them, enjoying their occasional reliance on authenticating narrators – in preference to the fancies of avowed fictionists – as responsible literary guides. Yet Scott knows no peer in his preoccupation with this mode of embedding. And in their most self-conscious form of persuasive rhetoric, his framing documentations are accompanied as well by many other insinuating stylistic hooks. Employing the voice of the obscure compiler and chronicler Peter Pattieson, editor of archival finds in their conscientious weaving together into colorful narrative, Scott's prefatory first chapter in the pseudonymously published *The Bride of Lammermoor* has its invented historian-editor worry at some length over the proper narrative modality of such writing – and, implicitly, the proper writing style for such storytelling. Masked as an argument about how to bring history to life, this preface is a prolegomenon on nothing less, as it were, than the value of style in fiction. From his own perspective as bardic poet as well as novelist, Scott rises to the occasion of this debate, in the subsequent first chapter, with a prose – very different from Austen's more restrained and pellucid classicism of the same period – operating in full view, or earshot, of British romanticism, including the enhanced value it has placed on natural harmonics not just as topic but as verbal contour.

Before this descriptive workout, and preparing for it, the rumination of Scott's prelude focuses on a friendly interlocution between the first-person narrator and his friend Tinto, the aptly named painter, who insists on the false, rather than true, contrast between the eye in painting and the ear in writing. The difference needn't reduce, he urges, to the rank alternatives of scenography versus dialogue. That brand of schematic thinking marks the difference, Tinto argues, only between painting and theater. Wedded to an aesthetic of depiction, Scott's polemical painter puts stress on the fact that words themselves have texturing capacities as evocative as color and stroke are to the eye – that indeed, at least implicitly, they have tints and tones and shadings all their own. Insistence on such a verbal optic narrows the gap between drawing and discourse – or, say, between brush and print font. The compiler/narrator pushes back, however, objecting that Tinto has "confounded the operations of the pencil and the pen," forgetting that "the serene and silent art, as painting has been called by one of our first living poets," is to be contrasted with literary art, which must be "addressed" to "the ear, for the purpose of exciting that interest which it could not attain through the medium of the eye."[6] What is unavoidable in this counterclaim, given Scott's prose, is that the "ear" includes more than quoted speech: more aurality to be listened in on in reading than found merely in overheard dialogue. Without explicitly calling up the mind's ear of rhyme and other euphony, this side of the debate is all being warmly ventriloquized, through Pattieson his stand-in, by Scott the popular narrative poet of often singsong rhyming couplets, now turned novelist.

The whole debate has been a kind of sidebar, almost a distraction. More important than the general priorities encouraged by Tinto, about the tints of prose itself, is the more broadly introduced polarity – and latent Romantic dialectic – between eye and ear in response to the scripted page. This interplay finds illustration in the opening moves of the coming narrative, even within the kind of *pro forma* genealogical backstory long ago familiar from the *Crusoe* model. This time, even the syllables collaborate with each other across whole phrasal spans – corroborating the palette chosen for this rendering, the landscape built up from the least syllabic dabs and flecks in the aural strokes of prose. In its historical ramifications, this takes longer to explain than simply to hear. Without mentioning the term as such, that opening chapter has been a debate about literary *style*. Only this dimension of the "ear" in literature can break the optical monopoly, subscribed to by Tinto, of eye and "mind's eye" together. For a balanced view of technique, in an economy of the rival or even sibling arts, it is not enough to level the dichotomy to a complacent parity. There is a third term that any narrative stylistics needs to have introduced. Between verbal sketching and cited talking, imagined viewing and imagined audition, there is the sound of the things actually looked at: words at work – as already apparent, for example, with the overworked internal echo and mimetic redundancy of Tinto's contempt for literary dialogue as "a *verbose* and *laborious* mode of composition" (37). Though of course the words are put into his mouth by none other than Scott, the "mode of composition" instanced there – in its scarcely pictorial but nonetheless sluggishly mimetic cross-hatching of both **alliteration** and long-*o* assonance – is oh-so-openly intoned as an instance of the implied third way between mute sketching and inscribed speech. In this sense, the sound of words, even though technically unheard, can still serve to herd meanings along melodic – or dissonant – lines of their own. These are words carried by typography but activated otherwise, in the reader's silent sounding of their phonetic shapes.

As the inaugural scene-setting of *Lammermoor* unfolds, no dialogue is needed to articulate in word sounds the force of historical decline, its inevitabilities and marginalizing pressures, as we enter the present time of narrative action. The setup is a kind of unostentatious Romantic poem in prose, an aural orchestration of what can be identified as the ruinesque mode. The inner turf of syllabification helps inflect the undulations of tonality throughout: "In the gorge of a pass or mountain gl*en*, asc*en*ding from the fertile plains of East Lothian, there stood in former times an ext*en*sive castle, of which only the ruins are now visible" (42). A similar internal recurrence is soon picked up again, in the philosophic cast of both an assonant and an alliterative inevitability, when describing how "their house had its revo*lu*tions, like all sub*lu*nary things" – with the nested echo actually reminding us of lunar circlings as the model for the shifting tides of fortune. We seem to have entered, briefly, upon a paradigm of cosmic recurrence in phonetic form. All earthly glory shall pass, and the manor house, scarcely exempt, "became greatly declined from its splendour about the middle of the 17th century" (42) – where the linking verb and past participle, rather than a simple **intransitive** form like "declined," aggravate the portrayed passivity of abjection over the course of time. Hard on the heels of the almost **oxymoronic** "greatly declined" (with the gnawing undertone of "declined from greatness"), the point is further rubbed in when "the last proprietor of Ravenswood Castle saw himself compelled to part with the ancient family seat," an idiomatic dead metaphor for the throne of ownership, "and to remove himself to a lonely and sea-beaten tower" (42). After the expanded **phonetic bracket** that ironically absorbs the contraction of status as well as of phrase – in the descent from "seat" to the passive "*sea*-beaten" – we find the dregs of the character's former ascendancy at an outpost, or region, ironically ennobled to the vocabulary of a landed realm: "A black *domain* of wild pasture-land surrounded their new residence, and formed the *remains* of their property" (42). Style does its work here via the vestiges of an already outmoded vocabulary of reign and mastery, where we all but hear, rather than see, the metalinguistic falling off from a Latinate vocabulary (the Anglo-French *demesne*, derived from the Latin *dominus*, lord). Privilege has plummeted into the everyday usage of remains, plural, in the sense of residue, in **back-formation** from the verb of biding or survival, *to remain*. History is as inexorable as etymology.

Now turn sideways, from the same year, to Scott's first English (rather than Scottish) setting for a novel, the medieval *Ivanhoe* – and to the first of what we might call its full-voiced descriptions of the midland forest: a phrasing in its own right so English as to sound like Wordsworth or Shelley in its extrapolation from the seen and heard to the spiritually sensed. Any repetition, sonorous or not, graphic or phonic, is owed to the stylistic binding of the passage, bringing the scene under the coherent perspective of editorial focus: "Hundreds of broad-headed, short-stemmed, wide-branched oaks" – marked with the spread of -*ed* attributes in a verbal exfoliation all its own – "which had witnessed perhaps the stately m*a*rch of the Roman soldiery, flung their gn*a*rled *a*rms over a thick c*a*rpet of the most delicious green sw*a*rd."[7] That's only the beginning of this middle-distance shot, which ultimately closes in, amid the stony ruins and assonant jumble of "Druidical superstition," on a single, half submerged monolithic remnant, an accidentally isolated menhir: "One large st*one* *on*ly had f*ou*nd its way to the b*o*ttom, and in st*op*ping the course of a small brook, which glided smoothly r*ou*nd the foot of the eminence, gave, by its *op*position, a fee*ble* voice of murmur to the *pl*acid and e*lse*-where s*ile*nt s*t*reamle*t*" (18). Anachronistically, in *Ivanhoe's* medieval setting, it's as if a new superstitious naturalism, captured in its aural register, has replaced the Druidical rites of worship. "Stopping" has been phonetically rephrased as "opposition" on the way to personifying the watercourse's role in this pl(acid) (fee)ble face-off: a soft arc of effect so whispered that it deploys the **onomatopoeia** of "murmur" (identified in the dictionaries as of "*imitative* origin"), in its internal syllabic ripple and purl, as part of an even more muted effect. For, in that oblique and tautological phrase "feeble voice of murmur" – in a perfectly rarefied use of the variously serviceable prepositions we've been noting – we find an almost textbook-clear instance of the **equative genitive** (the voice that *is* only a watery murmur): here in a reversible trope of barely noted personification. The phrasing operates just as subtly as its more logical (and inverted) formulation, *feeble murmur of voice*, would have done. Just as subtly, but – through the syntactic twist of logic – more persuasively.

Apart from the interpenetrating phrasal composite of what we might call grammatical figuration in that lulled genitive subordination, the attendant pattern of assonance returns with a vengeance, parodically undermotivated, in Dickens's first novelistic venture. It detonates there in a shotgun marriage with an inherited and travestied editorial framework willed to him, as it happens, by the same exploratory lineage of novelistic credentialing descendant from Defoe to Scott. No "imitative" sound here, except in its lampoon of an extravagant oratorical (as well as clerical or bureaucratic) circumlocution meant to *sound* better than anything it has to say in its ponderous syntactic marathon:

The first ray of light which illumines the gloom, and converts into a dazzling brilliancy that obscurity in which the earlier history of the public career of the immortal Pickwick would appear to be involved, is derived from the perusal of the following entry in the Transactions of the Pickwick Club, which the editor of these papers feels the highest pleasure in laying before his readers, as a proof of the careful attention, indefatigable assiduity, and nice discrimination, with which his search among the multifarious documents confided to him has been conducted.[8]

Done. Now on with it. Both homage and scourge at once, what one might wish to identify as the first sentence of Victorian novel writing has sprung free of its editorial precedents in the framing of fiction by sheer stylistic bombast. A new path is cleared, where phrasing like "illumines the gloom" will be taken up by prose melodrama rather than rhetorical satire and infused even further with the phonetic sediment (rather than lyric sentiment) of Romantic verse.

Well before Dickens, however, and four decades after Sterne, Jane Austen brought the novel to full realist maturity as a third-person, post-epistolary social form. She did this not least through her perfection of that **free indirect discourse** fashioned to report on dialogue without surrendering to its authority (in other words, by building in an ironic distance from it). One result is that she keeps her discourse free from the narrowing funnel of the epistolary first person that was a clear formal alternative (with an honored pedigree) at the time of her writing—and in which she herself began by experimenting. Instead, in her main fictions, omniscience gives her precisely the cognitive (ad)vantage she needs in this focalizing stylistic regard, from which she can swoop in and pilfer the idiolects of her satiric targets. A single example can call the whole breadth of her mastery to mind. In *Pride and Prejudice*, one Mrs. Phillips accepts the acquaintance of the pompous and self-serving Mr. Collins with a derivative cordiality. For "her civility was claimed towards Mr. Collins" exclusively "by Jane's introduction of him." Knowing as much, he tries wordily to capitalize on it, while narrational irony subsumes his words by travestied (which is simply to say cited) style: "She received him with her very best politeness, which he returned with as much more"[9] – indeed with the twice-as-much that strains the very capacities of free indirect discourse. Reported here is the unpunctuated gush of his unction – as if he were quoted directly in "apologizing for his intrusion, without any previous acquaintance with her, which he could not help flattering himself, however, might be justified by his relationship to the young ladies who introduced him to her notice" (44). It's like being there. "Mrs. Phillips was quite awed by such an excess of good breeding," and excess it is, with a bow and scrape in every piled-up scrap of doled-out diction. Pure (if tempered) "burlesque" – at a decided Olympian remove from Fielding's style of farce.

Audible here is what D. A. Miller calls the lordly "Stylothete" in Austen, borrowing the foibles of characterization without falling into identification with them.[10] Seldom, too, does Austen descend into wordplay of her own, phonetic or otherwise, though in her last finished novel, *Persuasion*, she is in high spirits enough to end with an uncharacteristic flourish of pun. To this we are treated when, two sentences from the end, we find the narrator making clear the long-standing allegorization of the hero's name in this second-time-around plot, he being the former one-who-got (who "went") away: "Anne was tenderness itself, and she had the full *worth* of it in Captain Went*worth*'s affection."[11] Tweaked in that fashion, the name suddenly sounds more like one of Dickens's epitomizing, or downright silly, surnames than like either the gentry's or the navy's credible nomenclature elsewhere in Austen. But nothing prevents its internal echo in this one sentence, across the given name and the chosen noun, from constituting a microplot of narration's own achieved amorous reciprocity at last. Such is the worth of style in its backshadowed final thrust.

So we can return, now, with whatever other associations may collect around his own surname, to the none-too-quick Pickwick and to the nonsensically hyperbolic revelation at the start of that novel, concerning how the minutes of his Club are to be congratulated for the way their informative prose finally "il*lum*ines the gloom" of a chronicler's uncertainty. In the rest of the nineteenth century, such cysts of assonance and alliteration, even in Dickens, are likely to be less tongue-in-check than heart in hand – or in Poe's prose, never "droll," always instead tortured, verging on the downright deranged. But, as we saw with Scott, sounds like this are in the air far earlier in the century, always prone to a kind of mitosis (or cloning) of their **vowel nucleus**. No horizontal, let alone bilateral, line of influence is claimed here, certainly, at this early "Victorian" stage in the transatlantic assimilation of Romantic sonority – and certainly not across the gulf between Poe's neogothic turbidity of style and the fulsome launch of Dickens's comic picaresque. Poe and Dickens each began their careers in the mid-1830s, and soon enough knew to read each other – and thus to come under a certain reciprocal influence. But this is before that, these earliest parallel exercises in phonemic bleed. Beyond matters of influence or genre, including the difference between an exaggeration essentially comic and one performatively neurasthenic and contorted, it is enough to note the separate power of assonance, its stylistic value, in the two writers' compositional instincts. Such habits involve a leaning toward internal rhyme exploited by each of the writers well before they could be imagined in any specific ways to echo each other: a gravitation toward such syllabic forms, yes, but only because of a deep instinct for the gravitational fields that such reverberations constitute in and of – and between – themselves. Almost by tautology in *Pickwick*, and certainly by circumlocution, editorial elucidation illumines a clerical obscurity and gloom. The aural magnetism of the very word "gloom," one of Poe's own favorites as well – as is the mood of psychic dejection named by that word – is more insistent and insinuating in his work. Yet if we were to designate the analysis of diction invited by the monosyllable "gloom" as part of a strictly lexical rather than an authorial stylistics, we'd be all the more equipped for tuning into its shared impulsions across such very different writers as Dickens and Poe, let alone Conrad coming.

Published as the novella is in the same year as *Pickwick Papers*, there are fourteen appearances of the root *gloom* (in substantive, adjectival, or adverbial form) in Poe's longest work, the *Narrative of Arthur Gordon Pym* (1837). Later and shorter stories could hardly be said to dilute such gloom, given their compressed scope, but rather to put it under stress from adjacent nuclear vowels. In the stormy seas of "MS. found in a Bottle," for instance, according to the whirring work of the *er/or* core, "all around were horror, and thick gloom, and a black sweltering desert of ebony,"[12] where the desert metaphor is only just that: a metaphor, or partial **metonymy**, drawing on the etymology of radical ocular evacuation in association with a blinding storm, accompanied by the further reverb, perhaps, of "roar" in "were horror." So engulfing is this turbulent gloom that assonance becomes contagious and inescapable. Such is the strength, the rhetorical hold, of this grounding noun sound. Then, too, and by no means incidentally – given the interpenetration of stylistic effects in Poe – the verbal texture of the passage is rendered denser yet by the congested, the palpably thickened, consonants of the cross-worded "thick gloom."

Nothing in writing like this trips off the tongue. Instead, everything seems caught in the throat of a unique linguistic paranoia, obliged here to a repetition whereby saying fails to police even the word borders on which it depends.

It is this faintly mimetic effect that is more fully worked out in the phonetic interlace – and performative commixing – of the talismanic word *gloom*'s appearance in the first sentence of "The Oval Portrait." Alliteration and its like, its distributed likenings, weave their initial spell: "The chateau into which my *v*alet had *vent*ured to make forcible *ent*rance, rather than permit me, in my desperately w*ou*nded condition, to pass a night in the open air, was one of those piles of commingled gl*oo*m and grandeur which have so long frowned among the Appennines, not less in fact than in the fancy of Mrs. Radcliffe."[13] It is the "wound" of "gloom" itself that must seek disinfection – but against all narrative odds. Allusion to the gothic novels of Radcliffe serves only to round out, and tag in explicit genre terms, the microgothic phonetic fretwork – of consonants this time, rather than vowels – on offer in "co*mm*ing*l*ed *gl*oom," taking its entwined place in a hybrid scene of "gloom and grandeur" whose terms fit snugly enough with Poe's aspiration for his own gruesome euphonies.

In "The Fall of the House of Usher," over half a dozen lugubrious appearances of "gloom" and "gloomy" generate a phonetic pattern that peaks midway, crystalized in a vocally abutted instance of "pecu*l*iar g*l*oom."[14] Surely that phrase alone, as who could miss, can be thought to offer the aesthetic of Poe's fiction in a self-involved assonant nutshell: an effect rounded on itself – beyond the consonant latch of c/g – by the phonetic chiasm of ul/loo. The noun form especially, "gloom" rather than "gloomily," as set off in its rueful monosyllable, can scarcely exist in Poe without vocalic reverb. In "The Premature Burial," as if to compensate for the foiled chime of that differently enunciated ure/ur thread of its own title, we hear of "the in*n*umerable images of g*l*oom which thus oppressed me in dreams."[15] Moreover, remembering Dickens's post-gothic and faux-melodramatic "illumines the gloom," we note that "illume" as verb is no stranger to Poe either, as when, in a particularly macabre scene in "The Masque of the Red Death," we're treated to "a br*a*zier of fire that projected its *rays*" – phonetic cause before effect – "through the tinted glass and so glaringly illu*m*ined the r*oom*."[16] Illumination in prose comes in this way, often enough, by the runnels of subvocal enunciation. Phonemes are recruited to picture atmospheric density and occlusion. Style is plot – or its dead ends.

And literary history hasn't heard the last of such flash points in "gloom" by the mid-nineteenth century. Part of its lexical use, its versatility, in Poe and later writers, comes, etymologically, from its kinship with the crepuscular darkening twilight tones of "gloam." Gloom can be inside the mind or out. A "gloomy day" entails less a **transferred epithet** than a nonmetaphoric description of lightless murk. Gloom can thus imply an objective correlative in the setting, natural or interior, for a whole range of darkening psychic states, moral and mortal alike. In negative terms, it is the perfect Romantic modifier: linking spirit to nature over the grave of vitality. In the political gothic of Joseph Conrad's *Heart of Darkness* (1898) at the end of the nineteenth century, the first cluster of the nearly dozen instances of the "gloom" stem, whether rendered adjectival or kept substantive in a nominalized blur of atmospheric image, sets in when five of them congregate around the shrouded, fog-encroaching, smog-laden vision of imperial London on whose river-of-no-return the discourse is first floated, even before the retrospective plot is launched. The momentary clarity of punctuation holds off "gloom" from its participial modifier and assonant ghost in the novel's second paragraph, where the syntax of the main clause, in the **double grammar** (as famously tracked in Shakespeare by William Empson),[17] of its evoked receding horizon leaves the adverb "still" tugged both ways at once in a vacillating syntactic slippage: "The air was dark above Gravesend, and farther back still seemed condensed" – is this syntactic condensation meant for "*farther back still* seemed" or "farther back *still seemed*"? – "into a mournful *gloom, brooding* motionless over the biggest, and the greatest, town on earth."[18] From there we get the now posited and free-floating "brooding gloom" twice repeated. Again, no debt to Poe need be adduced, but what we do note again is the coagulant phonetics registered in a single sentence – and this alongside its syntactic equivalent in lateral affinities and bifocal equivocations.

A monosyllabic noun and amplifying participle ("gloom, brooding"), in playing off each other at the level of their own vowel nuclei, are as much derived from a linguistic infrastructure as is, earlier in the sentence, the flanged grammar of "still" when deployed as both the temporal and the spatial intensifier "yet." Style is plot at this level, yes, but only as it plots out the interplay of its own syllabic and syntactic configurations. Nothing is too little to count as style, or begin adding up to it, cumulative, mutable, often elusive.

In casting ahead to Conrad as we've just done, we can arbitrarily round out a two-century arc in the exfoliating prose of prose fiction with his 1919 novel *The Arrow of Gold*, which happens to return, in the found manuscript tradition, to the documentary premise at the foundations of the genre in our 1719 example from Defoe. With its subtitle "A Story Between Two Notes," it is in the designated "First" of which, in the book's opening sentence, that we read – with none of the syntactic fuss we've seen before in such editorial flourishes – how "the pages which follow have been extracted from a pile of manuscript which was apparently meant for the eye of one woman only," who "seems to have been the writer's childhood's friend."[19] With the narrator sometimes suspected in criticism as another avatar of Conrad's favorite participant witness, Charlie Marlow, it is nevertheless the case here that the troubled oral discourse of recollection and evaluation organized by the frame tale of *Heart of Darkness* has been translated to a text not to be eavesdropped on, but to be read over the recipient's (or anonymous compiler's) shoulder. Yet this serves only to remind us that reading scribed words is always, in Conrad not least, an audiovisual experience.

In this respect, gloom again looms into familiar echoic earshot. To pick up on this is not to pad the career resumé of a word-sound so much as to emphasize again the resumption of its own vowel nucleus, or its adaptations, in varied contexts. The fact that the threatening verb "loom" has always hovered as both a graphic and phonetic specter at the heart of the word – a kind of internalized assonant cyst, one might say – is no doubt part of *gloom*'s dark charm, for Conrad at least as much as for native speakers. But the word's bracketing consonants can bring it into other magnetic fields as well. Certainly, this unnamed writer in *The Arrow of Gold* is another adept in the manipulation of the monosyllable. Of its several recurrences across the narrative, none is more dramatically foregrounded (by alliteration and context) than in the following negative (and titular) epiphany of an eroticized death moment propelled by slant rhymes: "Often I dreamed of her with white li*m*bs sh*imm*ering in the gl*oom* like a ny*m*ph" (283) – the silent *b*, along with the diphthongized *p*, doing a non-**plosive**, dreamy, unspoken phonetic work of the sort the fourth chapter will return us to in the bilingual prose linguistics of another emigré stylist of Slavic origins, the Russian (rather than Polish) Vladimir Nabokov.

As laid out before us in this earlier "dreamed ... gloom," Conrad's is a vision, as the sentence continues, "haunting a riot of foliage, and raising a perfect round arm to take an arrow of gold out of her hair to throw it at me by hand, like a dart" (283). As so often in this novelist's mastered but just slightly estranged English, there is the extra dimension of a fleeting double grammar in describing the eponymous golden arrow: "It came on, a whizzing trail of light," where the appositional phrase for the missile in flight, in its own right a vector of light, takes a split second to reach focus, even given the punctuation. Its actual grammar must flash into place after the more likely, or at least more immediate, sense of medium and vehicle at one in "came on a whizzing trail of light," with cause and effect in an instantaneous perceptual blend. And this only as further enhanced by the cross-worded **telescoping** at "of light," by a **fricative** drift, into the homophonic "of flight." It is the unlabored, however "haunted," intimacy of this prose that we find editorially repackaged – as, in its way, was *Crusoe* two centuries before, Scott and Dickens since, and Poe himself, not least with his "MS. Found in a Bottle": repackaged as transmitted documentary storytelling rather than fiction, bottling the flair of adventure under the auspices of historical disclosure. And lending "gloom," yet again, a sense of an obscurity not just ambient but textual, as in *Pickwick Papers*, that waits in Conrad's case for the hazy elucidations of style alone.

Gloom and its luminaries, then, in the long tradition of phonemic atmospherics. The literary-historical turn to prose fiction, or, in other words, the emergence of novelistic style – effected by writers as different as Defoe and Fielding – has given initial shape to our survey en route toward, and lately beyond, the Victorian advent of Dickensian prose and its American counterparts. No surprise, perhaps, that Dickens, in his restless phonetic variety, would find other and more dramatic uses as well, more closely anticipating Conrad's, for the doom-laden sound of "gloom" than just its lampooned hyperbole in *Pickwick*. When the embittered Edith in *Dombey and Son* is found "brooding gloomily,"[20] rather than "gloomily brooding," the thickening catch-in-the-throat at the *g*-ligature does almost as much mimetic work of morbid introversion as do the spaced-out double vowels. And long past the editorial fanfare that opens his first novel with a touted dispersal of archival "gloom," what does often cloud steady perception in Dickensian description is a barrage of stimuli that overcrowd it. It thus seems right to close this chapter with some taste of the even more ambitious grammatical drama (or, say again, grammatically figured intensity) that Dickens can achieve – quite apart from parody, but not from overelaboration – when enacting the very crush of sense impressions. And in whose kinetic intensities he builds on some of his own favorite eighteenth-century novelists.

Think of the flight from London in *Great Expectations*, schemed by Pip and Herbert, to save the repatriated convict Magwitch from the death penalty risked by his return to England. No part of the exit is easy, including the need to weave their way through the congested Thames in a small boat. Syntax is at first very much on their side, until obstacles converge, with boats blocking their passage once they, after a rapid "and" in transition, "were in among the tiers of shipping." So far: taut narrative grammar propelling the story along through a passage thick with description. But the reader hasn't seen anything yet – or heard its cacophony. After a few exchanges of dialogue, in which the sentiment of anxiety and dedication is ratcheted up, we return to what can only be thought of as a paragraph fragment, not just a choppy verbless sentence. Yet one balked, bulking syntactic span it is, for want of a better grammatical term, and no single stretch of wording could illustrate more clearly what I've often meant by calling Dickens the greatest "syntactician" of English narrative prose. In this prolonged **cumulative** buildup, cited whole below, phrasing's own restlessness takes the reader's breath away. The grammar's sinuous swerves begin with its own **slant rhyme** as hook, where the iambic "Again among" is found expanding, graphically and phonetically alike, upon the previous "in among" – until the *ng* sound takes on a life of its own. At this point it runs riot across impacted participles in their alternate verbal and adjectival forms, all charged with the ongoing, and with all subsidiary alliteration in tow – until this participial energy asserts itself further in absolute constructions (recalling our first sample in Woolf's "Mrs. Ramsay having died"): predicate fragments that work changes on the portrayed momentum by varying the forward motion of attempted escape with other kinds of "going":

Again among the tiers of shipping, *in and out*, avoid*ing* rusty chain-cables, frayed hempen hawsers and bobb*ing* buoys, sink*ing* for the moment float*ing* broken baskets, scatter*ing* float*ing* chips of wood and shav*ing*, cleav*ing* float*ing* scum of coal, *in and out*, under the figure-head of the John of Sunderland mak*ing* a speech to the winds (as is done by many Johns), and the Betsy of Yarmouth with a firm formality of bosom and her knobby eyes starting two inches out of her head; *in and out*, hammers *going in* ship-builders' yards, saws *going at* timber, clash*ing* engines *going at* things unknown, pumps *going in* leaky ships, capstans *going*, ships going *out to* sea, and unintelligible sea-creatures *roaring* curses *over* the bulwarks at respondent lightermen, *in and out* – *out* at last upon the clearer river, where the ships' boys might take their fenders in, no longer fishing in troubled waters with them over the side, and where the festooned sails might fly out to the wind.[21]

As the progressive verbal tense turns "for the moment" adjectival in form, one all but feels the double axis of seasick motion in "sink*ing* for the moment float*ing* baskets." Beyond that, in linguistic terms the entire paradigm of verbal equivalents, rather than being selected from expeditiously, is strung out along the narrative line: going *in, at,*

at, in, out. These prepositional adverbs – those littlest bits of grammar again, like the *of*s of Defoe, or the *upon*s and *into*s of Sterne –
getting varied momentarily with a new predicate phrase, "roaring …
over" – are then returned to the strictly prepositional "in and out"
for its third repetition in this under-schematized **anaphora**. Yet this
recurrence is then flipped by partial chiasm, in a sudden burst of
release, to "in and out – out at last," and the rhythm of "clearer river"
seems, in its own internal wave motion, to help break past even the
negated (but compact and climactic) *ing*-phrase "no longer fishing"
into the compound prepositional phrase that awaits. This new thrust
is now opposite in effect to the crunch of "in among," so that, at last,
the open sails "might fly *out to* the wind" – or, in other words, spread
to meet the breeze this very motion simultaneously responds to. And
if amid all this press of shipping, the phrasing "chips of wood" seems
a fractalizing detail, chips off the old ships, so be it.

A good number of this chapter's "technical" terms can be
reviewed by this checklist of semicoloned obstacles in Dickens's one
marathon – or overcrowded regatta – sentence: terms referenced in
the alphabetized inventory at the back of this book. One looks to
those *absolute constructions* leading a life of their own, accreting
as independent variables of the depicted action, even while pressed
forward by attendant *phonetic* effects ("clashing engines going at
things," with even "eng" taking its phantom part in this phrasal log-
jam); *assonance and alliteration* ("chain-cables, frayed"; "bobbing
buoys," "hempen hawsers,"); the *back-formation* (one part of speech
derived from its cognate other, here a substantive from a verb form)
that ties a second plural noun (in "chips of wood and *shavings*") to
the frictional action that generates them.[22]

More familiar rhetorical devices in this same passage, negotiating its semicolonnade of hurdles, include the partial *chiasm* of
release itself at "in and out – out upon"; the hint of *free indirect discourse*, dropped immediately in return to the cognitive overload of
omniscience, at "Again among," as if to say, on the part of the escap-
ees' choric voice, "Here we go again among the bigger ships"; the
cumulative syntax (in this case, amplified by nonfinite modification)
rather than *periodic* syntax that organizes the entire grammatical arc

by accretion and blockage, rather than suspension, even though its nautical crowding proceeds without an anchoring (pun allowed) kernel clause, floated instead on the beleaguered progressive tense of *ing*-participles; *genitive* ambivalence embedded with other effects, as in "cleaving floating scum of coal," whereby "coal" in itself is either distributed in pulverized form as the floating debris ("scum") that must be plowed through or is the source of some resultant filmy residue floating, and dispersed, more weightlessly as byproduct on the cloven surface; *iambic* rhythm (light followed by heavy stress) borrowed from the native beat of English verse either for lilt's own variable effects ("Again among the tiers of shipping, in and out" – a perfect iambic line) or for their balked opposite in an adverbial clot like that in the later emphatic iteration (and prepositional congestion) of "in and out, under."

In all this, an unspoken *idiom* (related here to dead metaphor) seems literalized: something like plot's "troubled waters." And the checklist of stylistic features continues: the internal (here *slant*) rhyme in "*firm form*ality" or in the final loosening up, via internal echo, for the metrical run of unstressed syllables pressing "out at last upon the cl*earer* ri*ver*"; the *mimetic* effects involved in sorting the passage in just this eddying manner; the drift toward *parataxis* in the whole prolonged fragment, where impressions abut one another without clear subordination; *personification* in the ship's figureheads, making speeches not just like "many Johns" but, in fact, like many political figureheads; the *phonemic* increments of syllabification breaking away from lexical borders into cross-word patterning, as, for instance, in the breath-heavy *plosive* sounds (what Dickens elsewhere calls an "air-gun" enunciation in the impulsive mouth of his character Fanny in *Little Dorrit*[23]) that end up securing a contrastive link, otherwise too distant for the binding of mere alliteration, from "*bobb*ing buoys" across the entire passage to "shi*ps' boys*"; the tactical deployment of other neutral or "filler" prepositions as variable locators in the whiplash of impressions, operating finally as the armature of a hinge phrasing in the final breakout from an implacable "in and out" to the unexpected "festooned" and the finally lyricized "out to." Poetic flourishes aside, however, the whole effect of this internally fissured sentence fragment, crowded, oppressive, distracting as it is, can be recognized as shaped by the "poetics" of sentence formation itself: grammar's own troping as the very figure of event in the prosecution both of narrative action and, as here, its prolonged transitional moments.

From which other figures, other metaphoric tropes, can issue in latent form. In the case of this – by any standard, madly overelaborated – passage from *Great Expectations*, which lifts free of its own congestion only when narrative (rather than merely descriptive) adventure catches hold again in the escape plot, we may well intuit a deep thematic propulsion. For beneath all the nautical surge and clamor, in reading we undergo nothing less, as if by tacit extended metaphor, than plot's *turning of its own tide* in the approach to violent climax. In this and all the other ways exemplified here, as we will continue to see, do the *microplots* of fiction thicken – as we steer our way to meaning across their often half-submerged currents of sound and sense. At this level of attention, meaning is always on implicit duty in the shapes and pace of wording. By the same token, an extra gesture of meaning is sometimes on hold in the unsaid of language's own free associations. Style is the name for the activation of either inferential field of force.

3 Stylistic Microplots
Melville to Miéville

In thinking about style, one is always starting over – with fresh evidence. Freshness, surprise, being often the point. And this can mean beginning, as in this chapter, with endings. Weighed in the balance of imagined action, the value of style can tip the scales in a novel's last moments. Even in verbally adventurous fiction, however, one cannot fully anticipate, early on, the degree of fireworks or fade-out that will be assigned to closure. Style earns its way as it goes, and dividends may be paid – and played – out in many forms. Plot can achieve its vanishing point in a dense horizon of rhetoric or taper off in understatement, closure secured either in the midst of verbal intensity or its wake. Only the narrative's particular verbal journey can set the terms of understanding for its point of rest.

Certainly no novel ever muted its way toward conclusion *less* than Herman Melville's *Moby Dick* (1851). Ahab's Pyrrhic victory is complete, the revenge of the whale's death taking the ship down with it. An unattributed choric voice, variant of free indirect discourse, transmits the last human remark: "The ship? Great God, where is the ship?"[1] The answer soon comes into visual focus across the phonic and syntactic interference at "*they through*": "Soon they through dim, bewildering mediums saw her sidelong fading phantom." In a minimally distended periodic suspension of that four-word impedance ("through *dim*, bewildering *med*iums," with dimness inherent ["dim"/"dium"] in the ocean mists and spray), the combined work of assonance and a further hint of chiastic syllabification ("dim"/"med") postpones revelation from "Soon they," across "through," to the verb "saw," followed by a sideways elongation of spectral alliterative modification in that "sidelong *f*ading *ph*antom." In this brief adjective chain, the pressure of alliteration is only a further horizontal nudge from the normal comma separation after "dim" to the almost adverbial force of "sidelong." And in all this, the point of vantage is a satellite craft soon to be sucked down with that ghostly vestige of the ship in a more aggressive whirlpool of phonetic recurrence: "And now, concentric circles seized the lone boat itself, and all its crew, and each floating oar, and every lance-pole ..." (576). Beyond (but rendered somehow more palpable by) the spin of alliteration, a merely graphic "anagram" seems implicit in "concentric circles seized" even before the suction sets in – as all but audited in the cross-word **sibilance** of the whirlpool ("circles_seized"). And the sentence has just begun. For only at this point, in a complex suspended syntax, completing the participial thrust of the roiled grammar so far, is the question "where is the ship?" really answered: there, where this last remnant, the splinter craft, is tending. Thus is the grip of that concentric funnel last seen – heard – in the very moment when its force, "spinning, animate and inanimate, all round and round in one vortex" as it does, "carried the smallest *chip* of the Pequod out of sight" (576). Recalling the fractalized "chips" of shipping in our last chapter's last passage from Dickens, call Melville's more dramatic effect a phonetic as well as material synecdoche.

Certainly sound play joins with syntactic byplay in the rest of Melville's finale. The now Biblical, now Shakespearean, now Miltonic cadences and convolutions of this novel reach their peak in an extraordinary last cadenza, sprung from an unorthodox plural and a multisyllabic adverbial neologism, "as the last *whelmings intermixingly* poured themselves over the sunken head" of the last defiant survivor. At just that instant, "a red arm and a hammer hovered backwardly uplifted in the open air, in the act of nailing the flag faster and yet faster to the subsiding spar" (576). Not the echoic "mast" again (balanced against "faster and yet faster") but merely its dwindling upper length, a thin remaining "spar"; and not a "backwardly uplifted hammer" but, more unnerving, the syntactically backward (as well as markedly Miltonic) **inversion** of "a hammer hovered backwardly uplifted."

The mimetic effect of this last assertive gesture is in fact so complete that it stands forth almost as a parable of tragic *loftiness* itself, a last vertical stand against descent. Accompanying this is the teasing anagrammatic ripple in the "ironical coincidings" of waving flag and ocean waves, where that epithet "ironical" seems designed as much to describe the convergences of a narrative destiny as it is to picture the irrelevant similitude that matches the flapping of fabric with undulating billows. In the process of such undulation, syntax could scarcely be more tightly leashed to action. Another heavily progressive *ing* form now arises out of normal grammatical sequence to secure an inner, graded assonance when the "sky-h*aw*k that t*au*ntingly had followed the main-truck do*w*nwards from its natural home" has its wing caught between hammer and vanishing mast. The resulting intensity, passing from animal pain to mortal desperation, is transferred by phonetic osmosis in the materialized affect of echo alone. For it is the living man, not the bird, who is said, in a phonetic bracket releasing its full discharge after an initial assonance, to be "feeling the e*there*al *thrill*" in an electric "death-gasp." This is the bird of "archangelic sh*riek*s" that, with its "imperial b*eak* thrust upwards, and his whole captive form folded in the flag of Ahab, went down with his ship" (576) – but not before the death cry has stretched "iek" out, eked it out from one syllable across two, into its phonetic apotheosis at just the moment of thematic explicitness for this vessel "would not sink to hell till she had dragged a living part of heaven along with her, and helmeted herself with it" (576).

In rounding out an extended passage thus bracketed in its aural whirlpool by "*whelm*ings" and "*helm*eted" for this no-longer-helmed ship, a set of gaping vowel sounds is propelled still by the *ing* churn that rims the Pequod's vortex in the novel's one-sentence last paragraph, dispatched in a simple semicoloned **compounding**. After a preceding paragraph beginning "And now," plot has come to its end: "N*o*w sm*all* f*ow*ls flew screaming over the yet y*aw*ning gulf; a sullen white surf beat against its steep sides; then *all* collapsed, and the great shr*ou*d of the sea rolled on as it rolled five th*ou*sand years ago" (576). Now is again forever – and the open-mouthed yawn of vowels has done its sixfold closural work. So, too, transhuman time is sustained in a continuity marked by refused phrasal variation: a raw wavelike recurrence that "rolled on" (the prepositional adverb of spatial pattern and temporal continuity alike) "as it rolled" – not "had rolled" – five millennia back: more of the immemorial same. At which point the internal rhyme of "thousand" with "shroud" offers only the last shudder of fate, in whose wake the final "as" – not of similitude, but of geological perpetuity – unrolls this last chapter's last half-dozen nearly neutralized words. The sunken vessel of plot has subsided into style alone: style, with its own alleviating contortions in the imperturbable onwardness, and sudden rhetorical subsidence, of its aural and grammatical undulation.

1851: an annus mirabilis in American letters. Witness the simultaneous publication of Melville's seagoing epic and Nathaniel Hawthorne's landlocked *House of the Seven Gables*, where, once again, a climactic death scene is a lightning rod for verbal discharge and its static electricity. Rather than sinking the protagonists out of sight in the lethal medium of their quest, this time a climactic moment locks a body tight in a domestic setting of *rigor mortis*. Yet style is no less vibrant in this latter case. This is because style, rhetoric, utterance itself, can sometimes flood a passage in ironic juxtaposition with, and even ontological disjunction from, the putative insentient muteness of its topic. When expressiveness slams up against silence, style *per se* – as the fullest evidence of human utterance – can thereby be thrown into unusual relief. Its value becomes purely differential, figure to the ground of oblivion. That's what happens in Hawthorne. The novel gives over an entire chapter to the stone-cold body of the discovered Judge Pyncheon: a villainous human form bombarded by rhetoric alone in an overkill of phrasal liveliness around the petrifaction of his dead body. The longer it takes to elaborate the facets of the judge's preternatural immobility, the farther style itself leaves his life deservedly behind. One can think of it as a kind of obverse prose mimesis. Paced by the narrator's extravagantly prolonged harangue over the insensate body, recurrently badgered by **apostrophe** to look to the man's trusted, indeed fetishized, chronometer and proceed with the busy, greedy day scheduled in his "memoranda," we are reminded of numerous abrogated plans and appointments.[2] Among the scenes vainly projected into the mind of the man's assumed momentary torpor – a mere "odd *fit* of ob*liv*ion"

(208), as the echoic prose has it – we gather the motive for his doctor's visit, conjured as if in the free indirect discourse of a still living intention: "Why, it is rather difficult to describe the symptoms. A mere dimness of sight and dizziness of brain, was it – or a disagreeable choking ... – or was it a pretty severe throbbing and kicking" – not just ticking – "of the heart." All the while, in counterpoint to this erstwhile urgency, "the twilight is glooming upward out of the corner of the room" (211), where that mounting, or mounding, of prepositions in "upward out of" seems doing its best – along with the odd intransitive form "to gloom" ("glooming") – to summon a sepulchral, rather than just diurnal, shade. It is a participle worthy of Poe and his suffusive glooms. And the very action of obscurity is now followed by oxymoron. In the diminished light of this rising shadow is glimpsed the comparable darkening pallor of the guessed corpse in "the swarthy whiteness – we shall venture to marry these ill-agreeing words – the swarthy whiteness of Judge Pyncheon's face" (211). Then, too, the only "throbbing" is no longer that of an overstrained heart but that of the heavily metered (or metronomic) beat in "this little, quiet, never-ceasing throb of Time's pulse" (211) that is accomplished and communicated by the unregarded watch. Peter Boxall, in his approach to the synchronization of narrative and human time in *The Value of the Novel* (as discussed in the Introduction, and within a philosophical framework provided by Paul Ricoeur), might well have instanced the judge's body, in contrast to the normal personae of "living" characters, as a sheer materiality made deliberately impenetrable, in this anomalous case, by any sympathetic projection of the reader via the apostrophizing narrator. In this way, the exaggerated exception might be thought to prove the rule of imaged bodies laid open to us across the contours of narrative duration.

As the passage presses forward, its assertion of Time does more than contrast with the pulse-free bulk of the rigidifying body. Indeed, we have already heard the following death knell across the quirk of wordplay in the choice "moment" for "concern": "Time all at once, appears to have become a matter of no moment with the judge" (212), a phrasing folded upon itself across the extra twitch of reversible synonyms. When its focal point is reduced to sheer insentient matter, that is, time is equally of no matter and no moment. Only the eponymous house seems alive to change, for those elusive symptoms of the thorax, never diagnosed in the missed appointment, seem transferred and depersonalized when the windy night "makes a vociferous but somewhat unint*elligible bell*owing" – and self-instanced iterative belling – "in its sooty throat (the big flue, we mean, of its wide chimney)" (212). A Dickensian **animism** is on tap to foreground the **personified** life of the house against that of the extinguished occupant. After narrative's nightlong vigil over the never quite acknowledged corpse, there is no resurrection to be had, only the belated wake-up call to beauty: "Rise up, Judge Pyncheon. The morning sunshine glimmers through the foliage, and, beautiful and holy as it is" – *foli/ful ... oly* – "shuns not to kindle up your face" (216). Athwart the rhythm of alliteration, the very word *sunshine*, scrambled and contracted to *shuns*, thereby arrives (somewhere between a phonetic bracket and a partial **anagram**) to shed the further harsh light of certainty on the chapter's goading diagnosis of the found body, where the impossibility of "up" in one phrasing seems shunted forward to redundancy in another with that contrastive "kindle up": an illumination only of dead matter. The prepositional cue that seemed to thicken the darkness now also summons the light of recognition.

Poe, Dickens, Melville, Hawthorne: all densely phonetic writers schooled in the sound play of a Romantic aesthetic from which they took their varying lessons and distances. Victorian is, of course, the British name for any number of such stylistic immersions and departures – and mutual influences. But such phonetic intuition follows no rules, no logical progression. Just as in the macroeconomics of social environments, the narrative environs of novelistic prose are characterized by their own version of uneven developments, as we've already amply seen – and not just marked by style in this regard, but motored by it. The stiffly authenticating voice that opens *Robinson Crusoe*, all labored subordination in its prepositional pointers, recurs at the start of *Pickwick Papers* over a century later. This is unmistakable – even though the influence, in between, of Romantic sonority on the diction of a writer like Scott (overleaping Austen's residual classicism) can also be sensed in assimilation in the assonance/alliteration nexus – the broad-band *sonation*, as it were – of Dickens's lampooned archival "gloom" in *Pickwick* (and the various sound play of his fourteen novels to follow) as well as of Poe's yet more obsessive hyperbole. It remains for the likes of Melville and Hawthorne to consolidate such effects of Poe's when subsumed to a more tragic, rather than gothic, vision that, however fevered, is stripped of all deliberate vocabular neurosis. Conrad's style can be thought to follow in this vein, rendering sound play ethically productive rather than merely psychosomatic.

TRANSFIGURINGS: THE LONG NINETEENTH CENTURY

But there are other strains in both senses, tests of coherence and lines of influence, that fill out the roster of nineteenth-century writing in a transatlantic mode of what is loosely called realism – so often admixed, as in Hawthorne most recently, with layerings of the gothic. When backing up just half a decade from Hawthorne and Melville, in order to look, in turn, half a century forward (1848–98), it is immediately revealing to compare two of the most famous first-person narratives – female narrators at that, both governesses – in two very different stylistic keys. Aligning Charlotte Brontë and Henry James in this way can help to appreciate not so much any shared devices of style but, rather, style's shared leverage in the heightening of prose melodrama.

At the point of crisis in 1848's *Jane Eyre*, the abyss of bigamy has opened. Rochester's living wife has been revealed. In recoil, Jane has taken off her own wedding dress, and only then realizes the full change this involves, pivoted around the clumsily, numbly repeated "now" and, in contrast, all that is no longer: "And *now* I thought: till *now* I had only heard, seen, moved – followed up and down where I was led or dragged – watched event rush on event, disclosure open beyond disclosure: but *now, I thought.*"[3] Brontë's habit of parallel expansions is seen in full operation in the shift from "event ... on event" – not to the expected "disclosure *upon* disclosure" (with its

tempting prepositional echo of "*up and* down") but, instead, phonetically as well as phrasally dilated, to the more spatialized vanishing point of "disclosure *open beyond* disclosure." With the result
here, or say "now," that the speaker must search for her own figurative corpse: "I was in my own room as usual ... And yet where was
the Jane Eyre of yesterday? – where was her life? – where were her
prospects?" *Nomen est omen*, in another homophonic variant: Jane
ere is now no more: "Jane Eyre, who had been an ardent, expectant
woman – almost a bride, was a cold, solitary girl again: her life was
pale; her prospects were desolate" – a dead metaphor immediately
expanded into an extended conceit of the "Christmas frost" that had
"come at midsummer" (261), as if in exfoliation of the unsaid metaphor of hopes nipped in the bud.

First-person rhetoric is an obvious means of focalizing sentiment.
What one might call the governing perspective of this first-person
writing is under stress from its own tropes. And sometimes, as at the
climax of Henry James's *The Turn of the Screw*, the narrative voice
can seem so warped by subjectivity that report veers between the
febrile and the repressed, with the very diction and syntax so dis-
torted by neurotic intensity that an air of hallucinatory blur invades
the entire scene. Terrorizing him to the point of heart failure, James's
unnamed governess wants young Miles to admit his awareness of
Quint's ghost – even as it is only the spreading and encompassing
projection of her own phrased consciousness, not the aura of the
spectral invader, that appears to engulf their shared space in the
very grammar of bafflement. Miles was "at me in a white rage" –
a phrase (almost paranoid in its own right) for merely staring "at"
me – "bewildered, glaring vainly over the place and missing wholly,
though it now, to my sense, filled the room like the taste of poison,
the wide overwhelming presence."[4] Swelling the periodic sentence,
in that strained grammatical interruption, is only the welling up of
the governess's own frenetic self-justification. Both **synesthesia** (in
that ambient taste of fatality) and alliteration (the cantilevered periodic span from "wholly" to its delayed phonetic traction in "wide
overwhelming") spread out the sense of evil, festering but attenuated, to a mere atmosphere of dread.

In the governess's deranged acquisitive triumph over the force of satanic pollution: "I have you ... but he has lost you forever." Yet that losing, next abstracted in her language as a palpable condition, is transferred to its true victim, Miles himself, constituting a fatal "stroke" of annihilation rather than a triumphant blow struck against the enemy. Prose begins registering Miles himself as "lost" in the maddened hammering metrics of the narrator's delayed recognition: "With the stroke of the loss I was so proud of he uttered the cry of a creature hurled over an abyss ..." (85). Though barely or ambiguously figurative in its own right ("[as if] the cry of a creature hurled"), the loss is further hedged by a seemingly conjectural "might" in the next clause – as if still levitated in simile: "and the grasp with which I recovered him might have been that of catching him in his fall." Within the vaporous subjunctive figuration, she "might" have caught and saved him, but didn't, for the abyss is real enough in one sense, and of her own making. We are returned now to the strictly literal, in fact the tragically material: "I caught him, yes, I held him ... but at the end of a minute I began to feel what it really was that I held," where the eventual "feel" of the rigidifying corpse, unsayable in her panic and grief, and dodged by lugubrious circumlocution ("what it really was that") is more literal than it at first sounds.

The sometimes excruciated nuance of Jamesian style, a fuss verging on obfuscation, an exactitude pursued to distraction, has found here the perfect vessel in the deranged fervor of his narrator. Whereas Brontë has her heroine work to figure an unmistakable anguish in the overt and encompassing metaphor of an unseasonable "frost" and its withering of "prospects," the governing tropes in James serve to buffer with simile and other deflections ("like the taste of poison," "might have been that of catching him") any clarity of mind in the telling. Never is it realized, from within the narrator's obsessive subjectivity, that the "wide overwhelming presence" has no plausible source but in her own projection. The work of figuration in these two governess tales, these two tellings, tends in just these ways to epitomize a radiating intensity of traumatic perception. Yet whereas Brontë has Jane wield a knowing trope drawn from the realm of blighted nature but by no means distorting her heroine's

view of the actual world that environs her grief, James's figure of
toxicity, and its implied self-contagion, vitiate reality itself for his
governess – and administer a lethal overdose of panic to the boy she
would save. Yet again, style is in each case a microplot in its own
right – and in the case of *The Turn of the Screw*, almost *the* microplot:
miniaturizing the entire logic of the novella in its bitter finish.

Between these two nineteenth-century narratives falls another
novella, more neogothic than either, that offers an even clearer
case of a stylistic turn operating as plot's concentration and precis.
Pivoted around the dead metaphor of "awaken" for *activate*, the
resultant double grammar of Robert Louis Stevenson's *doppelgänger*
plot in *Dr. Jekyll and Mr. Hyde* (1886) sets its central trope off in
style's precipitant rush across a **paratactic** comma splice – almost
a loosened biomedical suture – that can barely keep the two halves
of the sentence, let alone the alternate selves, separate. Grammar
lurches from a literal and intransitive description to a half-figurative,
half-transitive upshot, taking the monster within as the released
"accusative" object of a second verb: "I had gone to sleep Henry
Jekyll, I had awakened Edward Hyde."[5] Leaving consciousness *as*
(and then *of*) myself, I spawned my antithesis and secret sharer. The
dizzy reversals of this *gestalt* grammar trace syntax's own diagnosis
of the split subject, psychic before syntactic. The narrative distilla-
tions installed by style are rarely as dramatically compact as this, but
they are everywhere.

The last chapter recalled some of the loose and sinewy transforms
undergone by style in genre consolidations over literary-historical
time. Though far-flung in the remove of its settings and geopolitical
tensions, it is not so far-fetched to imagine, as we saw, the rhetorical hyperbole of Conrad's writing, with all its "brooding gloom,"
drawing on a hybrid strain of psychological melodrama and gothic in
earlier writing. And other lines of uneven and roundabout descent,
equally dependent on the nuances of diction, grammar, and figure,
can help to highlight the continued variances and values of style
in the proliferation of narrative form. Before Conrad's flexed complexities of diction and syntax, and earlier in the second half of the
Victorian century from which both his and James's prose would beat

their demanding retreats, we note next how fictional rhetoric crosses from Victorian realism into the varieties of turn-of-the-century decadence – and on through impressionism to modernist social critique – according to a similar leapfrogging of stylistic registers. It does so partly in open allusion and irony, always with a texturing impact on the shape of theme. To isolate but three examples of this further unevenness in stylistic experimentation, operating in widening historical arcs, we can look first to Walter Pater's burnished prose as it is sieved through the tighter mesh of Oscar Wilde's all but festering (if partly facetious) aestheticism in the novel *The Picture of Dorian Gray*. Reaching further back into the Victorian century, while also farther forward, we'll note how John Ruskin's mandarin symmetries, from mid-century, are submitted at the start of the next to the suave sardonic distancing of E. M. Forster. And in a farther-reaching trajectory, the emphatic repetitions in the sounding ethical rhythms that characterize George Eliot's reflective rhetoric, passed through the erotic ontological rhapsodies of D. H. Lawrence and their pulsing iterative beat, can be heard to return, mordantly undone, as if by a reductive compression of grammar and syllabification alike, in the dubious, half-stuttered predication of being in the clone narrative of Kazuo Ishiguro. All told, from Victorian humanist essayism, with its impact on the high realist novel spearheaded by Eliot and inherited by Forster, through the posthumanist libidinal mysticism of Lawrence, to the posthuman angst of Ishiguro's post-postmodernism, more metaphysical than metafictional, is a long reach indeed. And all the more so when we stretch forward as well into the stylistic ambivalence of another sci-fi parable in a work by China Miéville from just under half a decade later than Ishiguro's novel. Such stylistic continuities – or shared malleabilities – are broached here not to trace some eccentric literary history of covert dependencies and debts. Rather, rhetorical affinities and contrasts are raised to suggest how direct or oblique common denominators across writers, whatever one seeks to make of them, make their differential claims on perception through maneuvers of style.

Evaluation, whether in Barthes's sense of typology or otherwise, has in this way a new challenge. Once style has been given a certain deserved independence from the stories it weaves, a question arises. How far, short of parody, can writing press against its own enveloping effects in isolating them not just as functionally extreme, even downright excessive, but as actually suspect? Nowhere is the question better posed, and tested, than in the decadent moment of art for art's sake (make that style for style's sake) that takes its place in a broad turn-of-the-century phase of baroque prose – counter to naturalism's contemporaneous stringencies – extending from Wilde through James and Conrad to Lawrence and on, more lyrically inflected, to Woolf. The effects in the style of fiction are comparable, in this way at least, to the wrenching densities, as well as colloquial energies, introduced into poetic form in retreat from mainstream Victorianism's lucid verse euphony (Tennyson its standard-bearer), where, for the rival moderns, "make it new" amounted to "make it unrecognizable at first."

With Wilde, however, the distancing is more internal and elusive. Recall the opening of *The Picture of Dorian Gray* (1891), with its picture, first, of an aristocrat at his opulent leisure and ease. If judging the passage strictly on stylistic grounds, the undeniable beauty of its fleeting sensations, not obscurantist in the least, is shadowed by uneasiness none the less. Here, from the famous playwright, is a sustained flourish of rhetoric alone, no action, no dialogue, in which language's own massaging of hermetic sensuality turns the whole world into a narrow theater of feeling placed, by sheer style, under an autofocus microscope. Prose's own approximation of a "decadent" affect is, in fact, flagged by allusion to that classic touchstone of *fin de siècle* Victorian aestheticism in Walter Pater's *The Renaissance* (1873), with its celebration of the almost fever-pitch intensity of beauty's cult, a worship both material and spiritual: "To burn always with this hard gemlike flame, to maintain this ecstasy, is success in life,"[6] where the vocalic core of "flame" itself is sustained, in effect, across both syllables of its parallel **infinitives**, first by chiasm ("flame"/"maintain"), then, from within the flanged reversal, by internal rhyme ("maintain"). Yet sound effects like this, though very much under the unshowy control of rhetorical persuasion in Pater's crisp **apposition** and restatement, can, if more lavishly unleashed, turn indulgent, even tinny – or at least get thinned out to a kind tinsel scintillation.

As follows. In contrast to the self-fueled and self-consuming nature of the aesthetic ideal crystalized and enshrined in Pater, Wilde's ambivalent rendition of its inbred, narcissistic manifestation centers on – or so far, in the opening description, merely circles around – the person, and saturated focalization, of Lord Henry Wotton. This is the character soon to be skewered for the jaded skepticism of his influence over the eponymous hero, where the complacencies of his cynicism are as insidious as they are witty. We are not privy yet, of course, to this satire of the author's own *alter ego* in aristocratic phrase-making when we first meet him. Because meeting him is hardly the word for it. We are voyeurs operating with suspect access to the enhanced vision and audition of his own privacy, those hyper-attunements by which he seems to take in the world through the ephemera of its sensations, draining reality dry like the bees that at one moment casually preoccupy his notice. It is as if, for this inveterate verbal stylist, the world itself, as cognitively received, is all style in the lesser sense, all perceptual decoration.

The flame of unstinting self-realization is still fanned, but its gemlike rigidity has gone limp, as we are soon to discover, with over-indulged sarcasm and lassitude. Before we know any of this, however, we are pointed to Lord Henry's person *in situ*, the sybarite lounging in an artist's studio, a cognizant body not just located at, but musing on – so it would seem, via the implied free indirect discourse – the thin curtained border between nature and culture, each aestheticized to a fare-thee-well. In respect to the garden adjoining his place of respite, the allusion to Pater is almost the least of it, even when overtly summoning – with the intertextual "flamelike" – the lure of "the nearby laburnum, whose tremulous branches" (what else, in prose like this, could a "*laburnum*" be but "tre*mul*ous"?) "seemed hardly able to bear the burden of a beauty so flamelike as theirs."[7] Otherwise known as the "golden chain tree," the laburnum is a lush but highly poisonous plant that can induce coma if ingested. These effects are almost, in themselves, rendered symptomatic, by stylistic association, in the vaguely narcotized aura of the scene, as floated upon the cadences of prose itself.

The passage cannot help but prompt generalizations, which we can anticipate going in – and these directly in light of our evidence across the preceding two centuries of narrative rhetoric and its tonalities. Style is not simply a technical feature, a matter of narrative engineering. It is the interface, both tangible and impalpable at once, between plot and response. To begin with, there is nothing in prose depiction but words. In the end, or more to the point, in process, style is what those words *say* – beyond and beneath what they picture. They are more than the how, the means, of depiction. They are its manifested image in the sense of its figuration, its linguistic configuration. Style isn't the residue of setting or scene, of conjured space or action; it is the first layer, the front line, of reaction itself, the very prodding of response – sometimes its virtual model. Not just the representational *how* of constructed episodes, then, style delimits the *how we feel* in advance of what we think – and this very much in line with Altieri's claims about participatory affect in the Introduction.

In Wilde's case, when filtered through his exaggerated lounging surrogate, a sense of unearned satiety is redolent in the lazy libido of the self-pleasuring prose alone, quite apart from (or at least at one rhetorical remove from) its languid anchor in Lord Henry. So it is that the second sentence of *The Picture of Dorian Gray*, opening the second paragraph, gives us a prose suffused with the same effete delectation of the senses as the recumbent and half-numbed aesthete it describes. Something is so deliciously right with the world that its whole manifestation seems wrong, unreal, strained to the point of sensory dissociation. And the effect is carried by an odd spectrum of internal repetitions and redundancies that can strike us merely as casual intensifiers until recognized for the minor jolts they instill: first in syntax, then in diction, then in etymology, and then in definition. "From the corner of the divan of Persian saddle-bags on which he was lying, smoking, as was his custom, innumerable cigarettes, Lord Henry Wotton" makes his first appearance. The parallel participial grammar of "lying, smoking" is amplified and jostled at once by turning "smoking" into an overspecified transitive of duration ("as was his custom ... innumerable"), so that we are seeing not a body in action but a time-lapse image of his addictive torpor. It amounts, as linguistics would designate it, to the **iterative** mood of the participle.

And that time-lapse effect is next rendered visual by figuration and analogy, for this same Lord Henry, as the sentence continues – from his glimpse at the garden beyond the studio – "could," as anticipated, in the full pull of the flora's lethal seduction, "just catch the gleam" proffered by that synesthesia of "honey-sweet and honey-coloured blossoms" (7). Their luscious chromatic "burden" gives way in cognitive sequence, after a semicolon, to a loose cumulative grammar – with every flourish nourished on the insubstantial:

and now and then the fantastic shadows of birds in flight flitted across the long tussore-silk curtains that were stretched in front of the huge window, producing a kind of momentary Japanese effect, and making him think of those pallid, jade-faced painters of Tokyo who, through the medium of an art that is necessarily immobile, seek to convey the sense of swiftness and motion (7).

Effects thicken as action is forestalled – and even inverted. It is not only the painters who are themselves aestheticized ("jade-faced") – and so treated even in the subordinate grammar that specifies their skill (in the pallid assonance of "who through"). Further aestheticized is the passing recollection of an art whose uncanny ability to evoke the redundant "swiftness and motion" (stylistic **pleonasm** – as if to imply speed and "commotion," rush and flutter) is turned inside out, and thus further derealized, when real avian movement beyond the curtain, rendered "fantastic" behind this scrim, is figured to induce the image of its sheer ("tussore"-thin) imitation. Unreality rules, usurping the marginally removed event of flight by its idealized similitude. The truncated rarefaction of such a classic rhetorical effect as **hendiadys** – converting "the world's (the birds') swift motion" to its artificial components of "swiftness and motion" – is deployed here as if in the deliberate transcendence of logic by optic overload.

And if that was not enough to put the seal of decadence, or aesthetic retreat, on these impressionistic flashes, the paragraph is capped with a sentence that picks up, via immediate internal echo, on the earlier "burden" in a now strictly musical usage derived from the low-keyed personification that introduces the following new aura of airborne agents on the scene. Here is the "sullen murmur of the bees" – even the assonant "sullen" feels drawn into the etymologically "imitative" sound of "murmur" (as we recall from Scott) – "shouldering their way through the long unmown grass, or circling with monotonous insistence ..." We seem to hear the buzz in the responsive sibilance itself. Then, too, a kind of torpor is latent in the cause-versus-effect ambiguity of "long unmown" (neglected or lengthy). Moreover, compounding the widening byplay of consonants (via a loose phonetic bracket) from "(un)mown" into "monotonous," we are then told – we hear – that the "dim roar of London" was like the bourdon note of a distant organ" (7). The counterpoint of assonance is one thing, linked to the vague oxymoron of "dim roar" – and carried again on a chiasm of assonance ("oar ... don ... don ... or-") that no sooner brings the distant near than it distances it with simile. Cross-wired sensations shuttled across displaced epithets, blended impressions and oppressions – all converge in this haze of evocation. Beyond mere synesthesia, this is aesthesia rampant. Here is style as agency itself, operating in a sphere of perceptual detachment and rendered merely sensualist by the fumes and wisps – and whisperings – of a sense-making prose whose lucidity is itself diluted by the play and overlay of sound.

A very different and more explicit consideration of style puts into alignment, not Pater and Wilde, but an earlier Victorian aesthete and a later Edwardian ironist. In any attention to the valuation of style, one needs therefore to note, as we've just done, that there are moments in which, not by quotation but by performance, style can be in its own right tacitly – and sometimes openly – devalued: held to sudden account, shown wanting, or indulgently overextended. Dated habits of literary practice are certainly ripe for send-up in this respect. Dickens could blatantly lampoon the former mode of the "found manuscript" in all its lumbering editorial verifications. Beyond any such broad comedy, modernist writers may at any turn parody – by actual pastiche, as well as by "aesthetic distance," even ethical distance – their Victorian forebears. This happens when E. M. Forster, obviously gone to school with Ruskin in the formal symmetries and syntactic elegance of his own prose, puts the Master to a new test – at a far greater historical distance, of course, than Wilde's from Pater.

In the early phase of Forster's novel in which it appears, the cameo of Ruskin's prose is made to seem out of place in an unblinkered realist depiction of lower-class life hanging on over the abyss of civic nonentity. What is borrowed, trussed up, and then gutted in Forster's acerbic allusion rounds out an episode in class analysis that is actually an embedded essay on the social registers of English prose. A mistaken apprenticeship in Victorian High Style for one of his characters becomes, in recoil on Forster's part, a counter-primer of modern writing and its ironic revisionism. Where Pater comes dubiously bearing down, by intertext, on the sensory profusion of *Dorian Gray's* first scene, or first setting, so does that other burnished Victorian essayist, Ruskin, intercept the literary ambitions, as well as social abjection, of Forster's character Leonard Bast, underclass counter-hero of *Howards End*. Unlike the open allusion to Pater in Wilde, this turn in Forster's 1910 novel involves, finally, a sly bypass of citation so complete as to prove its internalization in the free indirect discourse of the character – and thus to close off its resonance in the echo chamber of a defeated sensibility. Yet the metastylistics of its irony, at this turn in the novel's prose, lays as many claims on attention as does the sadness of its plot.

The canonical backstory, from chapter two, book two, of *The Stones of Venice*, involves the surprising dead wall of the Venetian cemetery where one would expect, instead, an expansive lagoon vista, so that the venerable church of the "Misericordia" is abutted in the sentence, one phrase away, with its etymological echo in "a line of miserable houses": both an eyesore and an occlusion of the view.[8] Ruskin is no stranger to the syllabic principle that misery, like other word forms, loves company – and this euphonic understrain becomes an actual ethical strain in Forster's recycling of these crafted sentiments. For what we are to find in reading further into the Ruskin – and in this case to find ruminated at one remove, and regurgitated, by Forster's character – is that the Victorian writer is out to celebrate the fact that no squalid blight on the Venetian prospect, indeed no unabashed place of burial and grieving in a nearby graceless cemetery, can spoil the thrill of it all. Forster comes to this by allusion. The pivot point, in the subsequent transit from Torcello to Murano at the start of the essayist's third chapter, turns on the mandarin anaphora of this quintessential Ruskinian period: "Yet the power of Nature cannot be shortened by the folly, nor her beauty altogether saddened by the misery, of man" (33). How can polished symmetry like this, half a century later, find its way into the ramshackle life of a clerk in the squalid London precincts of Forster's novel?

Only by further discomfiture and literary misapplication. At a low point of frustration for Leonard in his dreary urban flat, even Forster's own prose seems off: "He drank a little tea, black and silent, that still survived upon an upper shelf."[9] Intake is as stale and "black" as his mood in this strangely divided compound, style itself out of sorts. Prose is beginning to dissociate from its circumstances even before, in a quite literal sense, Leonard loses himself – or wishes to – in his reading, studying the very different cadences of Ruskin as a model for his aspiring status as a creative writer rather than a mere scribing clerk: "Leonard was trying to form his style on Ruskin: he understood him to be the greatest master of English Prose," capital P. "He read forward steadily, occasionally making a few notes" (61). Then citation kicks in: "Let us consider a little each of these characters in succession, and first (for of the shafts enough has been said already), what is very peculiar to this church – its luminousness" (Ruskin, *The Stones of Venice*, II, ii, 23). But the Ruskin is immediately submitted to a mordant distancing by Forster in a passage of keen black comedy: "Was there anything to be learnt from this fine sentence?" (62). If so: "Could he adapt it to the needs of daily life?" In writing to his brother, for instance, a "lay-reader" in the clerical sense, might he say "Let us consider a little each of these characters in succession, and first (for of the absence of ventilation enough has been said already), what is very peculiar to this flat – its obscurity"? No, even the capping assonance ("peculiar ... obscurity," as if in echo of Ruskin's "peculiar ... luminousness") rings hollow: "Something told him that the modifications would not do; and that something, had he known it, was the spirit of English Prose." This time, the *spirit*, not the letter – which adapts to need: "'My flat is dark as well as stuffy.' Those were the words for him" (62).

"Style is the man himself," famously wrote, as noted earlier, the eighteenth-century *philosophe* Buffon. And the man, variously circumstanced, has, therefore, no final choice in his style. Ruskin wrote the way he did, saw the world in those euphonic symmetries, out of the lens (and filters) of privilege. It won't do for the Gissing-like naturalism to which Leonard might aspire as writer. Still focalized through Leonard's reverence for Victorian formality, however, we hear by further allusion, with Ruskin reduced to sheer "voice," how that "voice in the gon*do*la *roll*ed on, piping me*lod*iously of Effort and Self-Sacrifice, fu*ll of* high purpose, fu*ll of* beauty, fu*ll ev*en of sympathy and the *love* of men" – full of it, as we might now be tempted to say – "yet somehow eluding all that was actual and insistent in Leonard's *life*" (62). In the waterborne lapping of such effortless syllabic spans – *lof* / *lof* / *lev* / *lov* / *lif* / – one can perhaps hear a regrouped monosyllabic *love* sneaking in, by cross-word play, before being explicitly sounded and sidelined: a leisured love radically curtailed in its empathy, separated from the harder vowel of "life" and its deprivations. "For it was the voice of one who had never been dirty or hungry, and had not gue*ss*ed su*cce*ss*fully*" what these conditions might really be. The slightly fastidious syllabics of that sibilant demurral prepare us, in fact, for a plunge from contingent modifiers to the intractable categories themselves (as abstract nouns), including their own more urgent and jarring off rhyme – "never guessed," that is, "what d*irt* and hung*er ar*e" (62).

The Spirit of English (now post-Victorian) Prose is on the verge of its clinching irony at this turn, where the whole logic of free indirect discourse is wryly but stingingly reversed. We don't have to know, still less remember verbatim, the original passage from Ruskin to recognize its sheer sound. Ruskin is still afloat: "It occurred to him, as he *glided*" (together with the phonetic glissades of Forster's interpolating prose) "over the whispering *l*agoons," – and here a descent into actual recycled syntax – "that the power of Nature could not be shortened by the folly, nor her beauty altogether saddened by the misery, of such as Leonard" (67). Nature's sublimities diminish and outlast the lives of the powerless and squalid. So it is that the quest for stylistic imitation with which the Eminent Victorian has until now been read by the Edwardian acolyte in Leonard is converted to a reverse narcissism, excluding the apprentice reader from the sympathies of his favored text. And it is the tongue-in-cheek style of Forster's tweaked allusion that secures the point of both ethical and literary-historical irrelevance. It is no exaggeration to say that we find in this layered passage, in all its rhetorical sedimentation, the tacit archaeology of stylistic change itself.

At a different scale, of course, do we find the changes rung within a given passage – rung or refused, including the literary history that can sometimes be traced through the latter choice of invariance. Allusion, of course, is a form of repetition with a difference. Forster's summoning those formulations from Ruskin, in their sardonic discrepancy, is one deliberately vexed example. Other stricter iterations within a single prose episode call on other levels of recognition. Major writers at the height of their powers don't, at least at the sentence level, repeat themselves for no purpose. If there's a rhyme there's a reason. Style is its own mode of reasoning, and prose repetition its own mode of rhyme. And this is true no matter how blunt the chiming.

A philosophical novelist with an ear more for ideas than for music, or at least for the music of ideas rather than sheer grammatical melody, George Eliot is still willing to put unusual echoic strain on her prose at moments of spiritual intensity. Hers are likely to be repetitions-with-variation, the refaceting of a thought: often echoes with a second edge – even a homophonic pun in the least comic of circumstances, as when heroine and her estranged brother in *The Mill on the Floss* (1860), thrown together in the face of death by flood, have been emotionally reunited. In the moment of its own expenditure, a paradoxical sob of joy is expanded by the heavy emphatic elevation brought on by two appearances of *that* (one demonstrative, one subordinating) and a further phonetic echo – in a single sentence given over to a paragraph all its own: "Maggie could make no answer but a long, deep sob of *that* mysterious, *won*drous happiness *that* is *one* with pain."[10] The sentence chokes up with three accented monosyllables, then swells through the overstressed *ious/ous/ess* repetition, subsiding again into the last five monosyllables in their tightening from anapest to iamb.

Less melodramatically deployed than in *The Mill on the Floss*, an insistent lexical recurrence can, as later in *Middlemarch*, strike emphatic high notes in a sustained thematic of the moral imagination – and, in this respect, can look far ahead to an erotic solemnity of transcended self-interest in the very different but comparably iterative style of D. H. Lawrence. Across a broad gap between Victorian mores and modern sexual expressiveness, between Eliot's delicate if cerebral tact and Lawrence's percussive rhapsodies, these two disparate representatives of F. R. Leavis's *The Great Tradition* (1948) – its major standard-bearer among the Victorian sages and its wild outlier in modern sexual mythography – do meet after all on the common if unstable ground of a purposefully shifting grammar and its vocabular insistence. In each case, iterative prose operates to torque expectation into an emotional epiphany.

So it is that a late transfiguring moment from *Middlemarch* (1872) has its oblique way of prefiguring a quintessential node of transcendental sensuality half a century later in Lawrence's *Women in Love* (1922). The passage in Eliot conjures another and very different figurative "shipwreck" from that of her earlier novel. Drowning is here a strictly figurative trope for intense interpersonal immersion. The vain Rosamond Vincy, confronting the intuitive empathy of Dorothea Brooke in the famous Chapter 81, is released, under the magnetic pull of this nobler spirit, into the uncharted waters of self-sacrifice (Rosamond admitting that Will loves Dorothea, not her). Prose surges forward ambiguously for a moment – despite the grammatical earmark of punctuation – in evoking an impacted and transfusing newness: "Rosamond, taken hold of by an emotion stronger than her own – hurried along in a *new* movement which gave all things some *new*, awful, undefined aspect – ..."[11] An emphatic innovation of sentiment signals a moral uplift, but it is all too new a feeling to be given "definition" beyond its awestruck lack of precedent. All Rosamond can do, in letting it wash over her, is to go with the flow, though not quite. She is not the agent of the verb, it turns out, after all. Punctuated otherwise, the thought could have ended there, as quoted above. Smitten and inspired, she plunged into the moment and hurried forward: that would have been the sense. Instead, this serial and incremental grammatical insert on headlong motion, rounded off now in the remaining citation, gives way to a functional main verb after the realized passive format just before: "... *could find no words*, but involuntarily she put her lips to Dorothea's forehead which was very near her, and then for a minute the two women *clasped each other as if they had been in a shipwreck*" (491). It is as if the unsaid, propulsive *flood* of feeling has been figured retroactively by that crowning simile of survived drowning – derived as well from the "waves of her own sorrow" attributed to Dorothea just before, with that phrase's further tortured subordination in the tripled prepositional vector of "*from out of* which she was struggling to save another" (491).

In just this way, Eliot's prose has had to find the "words" for both women – and has done so, in part, by floating the momentary syntactic possibility of a spiritual impetus internalized in Rosamond's propelling herself forward with the energy of unwonted feeling. But the controlling grammar is immediately clarified as passive in its transfiguration at that point, with her newfound empathy being borne ahead involuntarily: "hurried," rather than hurrying, by the wavelike influx of another's emotional power. In fact, Rosamond is propelled so fast, into realms so untested, that even the adjective "new," as we've seen, can find no elegant variation – and is flatly (yet emphatically, transformatively) repeated in its registered cresting into feeling of the previously unforeseen. We may think of this as the stylistic rut of breakthrough itself. And measure its power, valuate its rhetoric, by how many words of commentary it takes to do any credit to the slippery compression of its momentary, if deceptive, double grammar.

Such repetitions and slippages are certainly the stock-in-trade of transfigurative rhetoric in the novels of Lawrence, where prose is often explicitly modeled on a mounting erotic tension and release. Half a century after *Middlemarch*, the intensity associated with such an enrapturing "newness" as Eliot conjures can seem not just revelatory but almost unhinged – even when phrasing the unfixed supple bond between lovers that is a given passage's rhetorical (that is, persuasive) burden. An overmastering emotion, as portrayed by Eliot, can certainly seem pitched to the brink of syntactic chaos in Lawrence – and held together only by an internal dialectic bent on enacting the erotic equipoise it strives to abstract and depict. The searing "newness" of affect has gone over entirely to a radical stylistic innovation, as if psychology and writing were equally obliged by Ezra Pound's imperative, not just to make it new, but to say so. Yet such is the flexibility of style that not just a similar device, but the very same word pattern, even when itself repeated, can generate a contextual freshness.

So it is that the redoubled "new" glimpsed symptomatically in *Middlemarch*, indexing a transformative experience too unprecedented and convulsive to be called anything else, is subsequently recruited by Lawrence to celebrate an erotic rather than – as in *The Mill on the Floss* or *Middlemarch* – a sibling or more vaguely sisterly bonding. This is the passionate affair, about to be celebrated by marriage, but first in the ceremony of prose itself, between Rupert and Ursula in *Women in Love*, as focalized mainly through the male partner's free indirect discourse. Interpersonal astonishment in *Middlemarch*, loosening the shackles of self-interest, and ultimately of self, now takes the form of coital liberation. "How could he say 'I' when he was something new and unknown, not himself at all?"[12] Carnal knowledge is only a new mode of mystery. With "knew and" hovering there like a canceled phantom echo ("knewn") – a fleeting homophonic pun slung across the chinks of syntax, active even while not activated – the "*new* a*n*d u*nknown*" is recapitulated at exactly the point of lift-off in the famous (notorious) next paragraph, begun in inflectional italics.

Let analysis take its own deep breath in tracing the contours of this syntax. "In the *new*, superfine bliss, a peace superseding knowledge" – with intensity stretched, across those unabashedly returning "super" prefixes, from qualitative fineness to quantitative overreach and run-on release – "there was no I and you, there was only the third, unrealised wonder." Under lexical pressure here, "unrealised" carries the sense both of previously unknown and of still inchoate, and this in a mounting phrase continued by an appositional repetition (that might have been borrowed directly from *The Mill on the Floss*) as "the wonder of existing not as oneself." Such is the won-der, in undertone, of the non-one, a fulfillment not as or of "oneself," that is, or even one self, "but in a consummation of my being and of her being in a new one, a new, paradisal unit regained from the duality." In the byplay between "being" as gerund and participle at once, even before the ambiguity of "new one" (as new "being" or new "oneness"), the genitive preposition arrives, in its double sense, to equivocate a phrase meaning both "a consummation made possible by our being separately transcended" and a "consummation of each of our singular beings achieved in just this transcendence." The former is a case (a grammatical case) – in Lawrence's actual phrasing, that is ("a consummation of my being and of her being in a new one") – of what is called, again, the equative genitive: a grammar not of action but of constitution, as in, say, the "passion of sex" (the passion that is sex). Fulfillment, in this sense, is defined as an achieved copresence in the new. This grammar's alternative, on offer in that same bivalve phrasing, is the more common "objective genitive," the consummation that takes (and remakes) its paired objects. Such is a self-exploding rapport between bodies in a new – who knew? – fusion of being, with the question still left hanging, grammatically, whether being is an entity (noun) or a process (participle). There is no telling – except for the reconfigured force field of style itself, which makes the new known on its own pulsing terms. It is in this way that two senses thus suspended in a double grammar, thrusting toward the resolution that syntax itself holds in abeyance, can enact – as microplot, yet again – the transcendental balancing act under investigation. There are no words for such a sexual moment, and nothing left but words, even as the pronouns that would anchor any predicated liberation dissolve before our ears.

CROSSING THE MILLENNIAL DIVIDE

The performative measure of prose amounts, in such cases, to a sense of writing's doing more with words than they seem to denominate: again, to their saying more than they mean. This can involve a rhythmic energy that ends up imitating, in Lawrence, for example, if not the actual rhythm of intercourse, then the building urge for an elucidating discourse about it – or, equally in Eliot, a search for the pulse-beat not just of speculative abstraction but of an ethics of the ineffable. It is in this way that style can be compared across quite disparate masters of its deployment for its funding energies themselves, whether manifested in the syncopated orchestral harmonics of a Victorian realist or a modernist erotic visionary – or held, elsewhere, in the examples coming, to the thinnest edge of effect in a more stringent reduction of affect. Let us say that the long nineteenth century has seen through to one asymptote of its humanist transfiguration in the orgasmic lyricism of D. H. Lawrence, with unstinted sexuality valorized on the altar of a humanism sacrificed to its new order of being. How can style, its grammar all but disintegrated in such a transfiguration, continue to follow the vicissitudes of "being" after a rhapsodic deconstruction like that? What is left for *logos*, for the work of wording, in grappling with a posthumanist ontology? In imagining such horizons of fictional prose, we can leap ahead to one post-postmodernist answer, or at least instance, in the mordant understatement of a contemporary fiction about artificially duplicated rather than transfused humanity. And in this respect, we can find in its exploration of cloning's depleted human autonomy a stylistic bifurcation not unrelated, in its grammatical waver, to the doubling of Dr. Jekyll by Mr. Hyde.

Repetition with a difference: the transformative power of ethical, sexual, and, here, biopolitical plateaus of human(oid) duration and finitude. We've so far seen how the monosyllable "new" can repeat itself without diminishing semantic returns, marking the limits of language to render without precedent, to name the unforeseen, to exceed all antecedence. Style is equally ready, in its minimal increments, to clock a passage toward its own foreclosure rather than breakthrough. No parts or particles of grammar are too minute or routine to be excluded from *part*icipation (the root sense) in the stylistic drama of fiction. In our probing the complexities of *Moby Dick*'s bravura finale at the start of this chapter, there was reason to mention the very different mode of closure that tapers and tails off, in style as well as content. We now have occasion, along an axis of existential dubiety, to instance it. The simple infinitive, the *to* form of the verb – identifying an action or condition isolated from time past, present, or to come, awaiting temporal specification in this way – can in the right context work to question both action and condition, agency, and being. This is especially the case when it is set off by other *to*-forms in the prepositional mold: thrown into relief, as it were, by false echo. Roman Jakobson's sense of equivalence projected into sequence, as the nature of the poetic function – a shaping of pattern beyond the needs of communication, turning the message back on itself as medium – is seen in the following passage from a renowned contemporary novel by Nobel laureate Kazuo Ishiguro, *Never Let Me Go* (2005), about the medium of DNA itself and its implications for genetic repetition. One might say that, in a last split-second pattern delivered under wraps in the last three words of the novel, the metaphysics of its premise is blueprinted by the grammar of predication itself: another microplot in action.

The fact of cloned lives shut down in their prime by premature "completion" (the technical term in the plot) is not only a trauma for these biological subjects but a challenge for closure in the novel form. The book in fact ends with the female narrator, stopped in the middle of nowhere, allegorizing a scene of trash and loose vegetation found collecting against a windswept fence as if this untraversable barrier figures the point of no return for the snagged, glimpsed details of her vanishing life. There is no crossing over to retrieve it, nor them – neither the life, nor its random details. Altogether, there is no going back. In contrast, the going forward feels not just spatiotemporal, but ontological – and potentially evacuated, or at least equivocated, as such. In the last sentence, with the heroine not knowing "where I was" exactly at this point of reverie, "I just waited a bit, then turned back to the car, to drive off to wherever it was I was supposed to be."[13]

The downbeat flatness of this finish has an extra beat or two of suggestion when reread, as it almost inevitably will be, the sentence thrown back on its own resources by the sudden truncating blankness of the remaining page. In the flexion of that prepositional phrase giving way on the slant to the *to* of the infinitive, the stumble of the grammar momentarily disrupts a reader's sense of rhythm and direction, its affectless lumpiness capturing in turn the frailty of the cloned *self* as well as the arbitrary contingency of her obligations. Plot is over, as we can tell from the looming blank space beyond the last line of print. What is left pending, exactly? Is the aftermath intended in the form of *to drive ... to wherever ... I was next, in the scheme of things, meant to be?* What about the momentary warp induced by "to drive to wherever *it was I was ...*"? Is this rightly felt as a symptomatic glitch in the iterated verb of being? And in that case doesn't "wherever I was supposed to be" convey the merely conjectural nature of her being in the first place – with existence for this derivative organism being only dubious and suppositional ("supposed to be") at best? The only answer: the blank space of the unwritten stretched out after *to be*, backed up as this infinitive is against the no longer inbred, but instead genetically engineered and strategically truncated, fact of organic finitude.

And after our long arc forward from intermixed forms of melodrama and gothic to an austere and cerebral science-fiction novel like *Never Let Me Go*, we can close with another and more mysterious variant of the genre, even more dependent for its initial clues on the prestidigitations of style. In contemporary British writer China Miéville's multi-awardwinning 2009 novel *The City & the City*, the ampersand has a way of inscribing the involute nature of the titular conjunction: a mostly impervious reciprocal relation between the alternate realities of the European metropolises of Besźel and Ul Qoma. These are densely inhabited spaces geographically coterminous with, but typically invisible to, each other in their separate languages and "crosshatched" urban zones. None of this is known to the reader, or even glimpsed in embryo, for most of the first chapter. Only just before the chapter closes – and the plot thickens, the microplot with it – does the return of the narrator's own repressed knowledge of the doubled Other begin to surface. It emerges precisely at the cusp between "protuberance" (or "protub," where one world bursts into the consciousness of the other) and sheer hallucination, for only at the bulging forth of alterity into present continuity is the ghostly presence of the parallel reality made known. The terms by which to understand this come forth only later. So far, it is the work of style alone to adumbrate this "breach" of the "interstice" (key terms for the bizarrely coupled ontology of these worlds). The first chapter closes, that is, by doing no more than opening faintly upon the uncanny nature of this (un)heimlich (yet weirdly hometown) doubleness. Yet by way of normalizing the mystery or explaining away its preternatural qualities, we're not in the least closer to a rational explanation by the closing sentence of the whole novel: "I live in the interstice yes, but I live in both the city and the city."[14] Affirmation is all there is of bilocation, hence the unpunctuated "yes," with its further overtone of some twice-sounded elongated plural ("interstice[sye]s") for the many transgressive interspaces of the novel. With this phrasing followed there, as it is, by that quotidian discursive touch of "both ... and," we recognize a logical formula that hardly does justice to the destabilized neither/nor of the plot's reversible virtualities.

If style is our guide here, it lures us into the imponderable at the level of the most everyday turns of phrase and cognition. Earlier in the novel, we have seen the time/space interleaving of the two civic zones figured in explicitly grammatical terms, where "Copula Hall" – as transit point between realms ("copula" the verb of being itself, often a so-called "linking" verb) – is "shaped like the waist of an hour glass": a "funnel" of "ingress" and "egress" alike, "letting visitors from one city into the other, and from the other into the one" (70). The thought was complete before those last seven words, whose redundant version of "the latter into the former" – with words as redundant to each other as the two cohabiting populations – collapses instead into the oxymoronic ontology of two-as-one. It is as if words are permitted to play subliminal tricks on consciousness that grow comparable to, and perhaps help model, the double vision necessary to accede to the novel's tacit sociopolitical premise: the lapse of mutuality and recognition in modern communal existence. At a moment like this, the sense of a warped idiom from a narrator communicating in a language not native to him, an English far less "polysemous" in its diction that his mother tongue (Besźt), makes every linguistic wrinkle all the more responsive to the plot's metaphysical double fold.

In the spirit of our Introduction, again we may ask, and perhaps never more pointedly than with such a fiction: *style as opposed to what?* A fiction, that is, where even the technical term "polysemous" bears overtones of a syllabic pun on a sutured and cross-*seamed* reality in a theater of collective denial. The least little tucks – even ruptures – of style can make this metastylistic dimension seem unmistakable. In leaving the police interview at the end of the opening chapter, the narrator is walking down a street with trash at the far end. "It might be anywhere" (12), this debris, since rubbish, we later find out, is all that these twin cities openly share, rendered indistinguishable as to source or ownership in the very process of its decomposition. But now the alternate human reality obtrudes, protrudes, penetrates. This happens when an "elderly woman was walking slowly away from me in a shambling sway," where the expected "way" appears varied, doubled, by the alliterating "sway." Split vision seems inculcated at the level of diction *per se* in its tracked syntactic sequence. When she looks in his direction, as if knowingly *at* him, he is "struck" – ordinarily the deadest of metaphors, if not quite here – by her motion, "and I met her eyes." English colloquialism is foregrounded and estranged just slightly, yet again. Rather than the idiomatic reciprocity of "our eyes met," the actual phrasing ("I met her eyes") seems a balked **synecdoche** for human encounter. There is certainly nothing markedly rhetorical about this prose; all operates in the vein of police procedural, if not quite in the mode of a hard-boiled detective genre. Yet surprises happen, as with this meeting without greeting, this exchange where certainly "no I's met" – across how wide, or how infinitesimal, a gulf, we are still, in the first chapter, left guessing.

Hints mount stylistically, however, including the coming first appearance of an Orwell-like version of Newspeak in the negative of notice (to "unnotice"). Nothing rhetorical here, either, but verbal tension is exerted at precisely the highlighted border between syntactic election and grammatical license. "In my glance I took in her clothes, her way of walking, of holding herself, and looking" (12). The stair-step **parallelism**, a kind of broken anaphora, condenses toward that third, awkwardly freestanding gerund, without the previous guiding preposition. The effect is thus to stress again, by indirection, the juncture of subject and object in a momentary "looking" that must soon be undone, since "I *shouldn't* have seen her": a subjunctive both epistemological and societal, given the political mandate of mutual oblivion on both sides of the "Copula" – or, as we're beginning to sense even here, on both sides of the very predication of being at the Besźel/UlQoma interface. For this is where people project onto their urban *alter ego*s, even in moments of transgression, with the vigilance of cinematic disavowal, thus requiring the continuous veto – or at least rapid deflection – of any acknowledged gaze across the invisible fourth wall.

The next paragraph lurches back with a double abruptness, narrative and grammatical: "Immediately and flustered" – the modifiers oddly abutted – "I looked away, and so did she, with the same speed" (12). We don't say the likes of "Eagerly and flabbergasted, I accepted her offer." At least a disjunctive "but" would be necessary to standardize this. Grammatically acceptable though it may legally be, the syntactic logic of "immediately and flustered" bestrides a miniscule chasm that has fashioned itself rather directly on theme. Phrasing appears here as a muted version of **syllepsis** in modification rather than predication, where, instead of two senses of a verb forking between separate objects, in this case the syntactic division of labor (and this at an interface between incompatible topographies) is between adverb and past-participial adjective. The very moment must be curtailed and buried, with the chapter then closing in an interstitial grammar all its own, as we'll see next: unpunctuated precisely to speed its phrasing under the wheels of erasure almost as soon as a given possibility is formulated. The split universe of alternately realized city-states has found its linguistic allegory – its microplot – not just in "polysemous" diction but in the shunts of double grammar itself and the skewed idioms it recruits.

Ishiguro on the cloned organism; Miéville on the cloned social subject – each in their cloven realities (like syllepsis given material form) forking open a conceptual space in existence itself. So the question abides: style as opposed to what? We've noted before, when prompted by evidence, the operation of grammar as figure, including its directly mimetic dimension. Here, in Miéville, linguistics figures ontology at a deeper level: the being of language all told, in its very multi-ply nature, serving the split language of being. Including the rudimentary grammar of negation, in the now-you-see-it-now-you-don't mode. Triggered at this turn is that Orwellian negative antici-pated above – an unflagged neologism in its own right, easy to miss on first reading, given its counterintuitive grammar: "When after some seconds I looked back up, *un*noticing the old woman stepping heavily away, I looked carefully instead of at her in her foreign street at the *facades*" (emphasis added) of the buildings: a facingness safer than the alien face. If the assonance of "stepping heavily" prepares for "instead," nothing prepares for the grammatical kink of the lat-ter's own deployment. The normative "I looked carefully instead at" is reformatted by a long adverbial interruption, unpunctuated, unpunctual – disruptive and thus immediately beaten back – across the breached cadence of "I looked carefully *instead of at her in her foreign street* at the facades …" Rather than a controlled pause, here again is a more drastic "protub" in a small-scale periodic grammar of the overtaxed interstice. Never, perhaps, has a simple awkwardness of syntactic pacing, or call it a warp in syntactic timing, done more work.

Thus does the first chapter of *The City & the City* begin to let loose its mystery – in the slackened or knotted ligatures of prose before the further revelations of narrative. In many earlier examples from the phrasal microplots of our present chapter as well, from centuries one or two back, the effects taken under advisement by response and analysis – pulled as they are between rule and extruded departure, doxa and eccentricity, normative verbal "façade" and its resistant interface – have been quite literally *telltale*. Plot's least, if not always first, moves can seem generated when a given phrasing, often playing upon its own phonetic basis, is taken to vacillate in just these ways between law and license, system and deviance, language base and instanced phrasing, the grammar and the syntax.

4 A Rhetorical Spectrum
Wharton, Woolf, Waugh, Wallace, and Beyond

There is another way, now, to articulate the questions that have spurred the examples so far. How does style dial-in and fine-tune – ultimately evaluate – the rhetorical stance that actively enlists it, in everything from bitter tragic solemnity to celebration to satire, elegiac fade-out to epiphanic lift-off to sarcastic barb? And with what plausible variety across the whole range of modern and postmodern writers whose prose possibilities can be recognized as unshackled precisely by the decadent and impressionist breakthroughs at the turn of the nineteenth century? When Lily Bart's drug overdose in Edith Wharton's *The House of Mirth* (1905) is ferrying her to oblivion, style catches not only the lulling of cognition in the whispers of sibilance but also the last spasm of panic. We hear, first, that all worry "was gradually lost in an indistinct sense of drowsy peace": a double genitive, with "sense" being both "drowsy" in itself, quiescent, and vanishingly aware of itself as such. Tracked by sound and sense together is a dimming of mind "through which, *of* a sudden, a dark flash *of* loneliness and *terror tore* its way."[1] Here it is the first disruptive and idiomatic preposition "of" (as in "*all* of a sudden") that imparts so new and wrenching a lurch to the prose that the key-word of dread, no sooner emerging from a compound grammatical bond with isolation (in the faintly bracketing assonance of "loneliness and terror"), is then sped to its own impacted phonetic and word-rending telescopic compression in "*terror to*re" (335)—as if the homophonic *tear* of trauma were ripping open the noun itself.

But short of insisting on a coordinated mimetic syntax articulating this last crisis for the heroine, what, more generally, are the effects of rhetoric, in terms of persuasive reader investment, micromanaged by such stylistic intensity? Questions like this are by no means merely rhetorical, at least once the rhetorical stance in question is specified – and identified all the more clearly by contrast with certain decided alternatives, to be examined next, in the further difference between the often rhapsodic stream of consciousness in Virginia Woolf and the extravagant satiric discourse of her younger contemporary Evelyn Waugh. We've seen in the Introduction the weight of mordant syntactic understatement, with none of Wharton's fierce immediacy, in one of Woolf's most arresting ex post fact death scenes. How, in contrast, can style alone enshrine and vitalize the quality of life thus lost? More specifically: whereas Mrs. Ramsay dies suddenly in the "Time Passes" section of *To The Lighthouse*, how in the previous novel, *Mrs. Dalloway* (1925), does the eponymous heroine submerge herself in the medium of time passing across a very different pacing of syntax, figuration, and, once again, those most miniscule of orienting lexemes known as prepositions?

Big Ben has just elated Mrs. Dalloway, out shopping among the London crowds, first with its induced communal suspense before striking, then with its bold sounding: "There! Out it boomed."[2] That rapid, compact inversion works as if it were responding to the very air pressure of sound waves even before the onomatopoeia of their designation as a "boom," then glossed by an ensuing metrics of description: "First a warning, musi*cal*; then the hour, irrevo*cable*" – a phrasing marked by that associated widening (of vowel sound as well as phonetic bracket) from *cal* to *cable*. Before the figurative pressure of the resulting "*leaden* circles" is said to have "dissolved in the air," that unlikely transferred epithet seems borrowed by displacement from the materiality of the resonance in question – even, by further association, from the unseen circular shape of the metal bell itself: displaced outward in attenuation, that is, to the heavy concentric *rings* (one residual sense only, in "circles," though almost a pun on the sound they figure) in a kind of acoustic lingering. The passage is saturated almost beyond containment with the sonority it evokes. The actual linguistic term "vocable" broached in the phonic hint of "*ear*revocable" is followed by two cross-word (rather than cross-syllable) reverbs, first in the "susp*en*se before Big B*en* strikes," then in the muted echoic "din" of "lea*den* circles dissolve*d in* the air," where the last described attenuation also seems to offer its own vocalic thinning-out, in "the air," of the exclamatory "There!"

This undertone of punning echo continues into the immediately following litany of London energy: "In people's eyes, in the swing, tramp, and trudge; in the *bell*ow and the uproar ... " (4) With the passing mimetic confusion further at play in the hint of "below" against the "up" of this invigorating "roar," Woolf begins a single rippling sentence that ends, after a further list of *in*-governed "carriages, motor cars, omnibuses, vans, sandwich men shuffling and swinging; brass bands; barrel organs," and so forth, not in the grammatical closure of any expected inverted predication that would organize the "in" in some standard fashion. Instead of something like "in all this she took delight," the syntax is foreshortened to "was what she loved" – and then the summary appositions: "life; London; this moment of June."

What's in a word? And what sort of word is *in* there? Climaxing the discrepant check list of convergent invigorations whose very diversity is Woolf's point, the crowding of random, *in*-determinate buildup ends by infiltrating the syllabic shape of the very entities enlisted in this harmonized vision. For, in alternating league with a long-*i* rhyme, the foregoing features of the June day are climaxed "*in* the tr*i*umph and the j*i*ngle and the strange h*i*gh s*i*ng*i*ng of some aeroplane" – as this last compound and mounting prepositional phrase finally reaches forward to the delayed predicate in "was what she loved." Not these things in themselves, but something in them, more inherent. Call it the pervasive ontology of the "life" itself they both populate and constitute in their dailiness. The rhythm of style is foregrounded, at such moments, in the process of its own exercised (as well as exemplified) valuations. In the same prepositional spirit as Wordsworth, in Woolf it is by the right mental language that we "see into the life of things."[3] Or put it that, beneath the stream of consciousness that her prose brings to unprecedented finesse, eddies the linguistic unconscious of her own enunciations: the existential predications on which they depend.

In contrast to such ontological embrace, the grammar of enunciation is of equal service, of course, in effecting sarcastic distance and misanthropic irony. In this regard, one can look ahead three years to Evelyn Waugh's famously ungenerous – and often cited as ethnically contemptuous – portrait of the Welsh band in his first novel, 1928's *Decline and Fall*, the title alone suggesting that the British empire, rather than the Wales hinterlands, will bear the brunt of the satire. Unlike the rolling list of the *Mrs. Dalloway* passage, here parallel grammar tightens the noose of revulsion rather than empathy, but all as filtered through – and focalized by – the implicit lens of a ludicrous upper-class British snobbery under simultaneous lampoon. Such a sentence would normally have served: The shambling band members were low-browed and crafty-eyed as they approached on crooked limbs. Instead, we are introduced to this unflattering tableau with a carefully chosen tinny numerical rhyme: "T*en* m*en* of revolting appearance were approaching from the drive" – approaching, that is, as the anchoring spatial as well as emotive point of view of their progress, a gentrified gathering of British administrators at a posh private school. Taking shape in a kind of choric free indirect discourse, the ensuing parallelism is as snooty in form as the attitude is patronizing: "They were low of brow, crafty of eye, and crooked of limb,"[4] everything the high-toned balanced syntax of the prose is meant to distance itself from. More devolved even than Neanderthals, it would seem, "they advanced huddled together with the loping tread of wolves, peering about them furtively as they came, as though in constant terror of ambush; they slavered at their mouths, which hung loosely over their receding chins, while each clutched under his ape-like arm a burden of curious and unaccountable shape" (278). These last are their dubious instruments, mocked along with their persons in the phobic euphonies of Waugh's tongue-in-cheek recoil. With the intruders lupine and apish at once, figuration founders on its own excess (as with Fielding's conflation of "tigress" and "pike" in Chapter 2), just as the stilted grammar preceding it had boomeranged into self-parody. Style, we might say, is keeping the contemptuous rhetoric honest in its wholesale send-up. However outrageous, this is what makes it funny.

Moreover, this kind of satiric denigration has cut its teeth on the imperial Brits themselves in the novel's opening chapter. There, in a

clear case of free indirect discourse, the narrative is channeling the
jaded revelers at the annual "beano" (or bash) of a degenerate Oxford
club, where the previous iteration of this Bollinger dinner is recalled
for the highlight of its festivities, when "a fox had been brought in a
cage, and stoned to death with champagne bottles. What an evening
that had been!" (233). A fox hunt without the horses or hounds: privilege in a reductive and extreme key. After a year's understandable
respite, the Club's celebration is on again, with the town gorged by
returning members, including, in one disreputable series, "epileptic
royalty from their villas of exile; uncouth peers from crumbing country seats; smooth young men of uncertain tastes from embassies and
legations; illiterate lairds from wet granite hovels in the Highlands"
(233). In this riot of leveling alliteration, a mild syllepsis is introduced
for the next listed parties, their sexual tastes perhaps less "uncertain" than those "sm*ooth*" (rather than "unc*outh*") "young men"
recently enrolled on the guest list. For, in two different figurative
senses, the newest celebrants have been yanked away from the social
swirl and the clutches of flirtation alike: namely, "those ambitious
young barristers and Conservative candidates torn from the London
season and the indelicate advances of debutantes" (233). In sum, next
and last, and in another slight forking (or redundancy) in the scope of
the euphonious, "all that was most sonorous of name and title was
there for the beano." Whatever a resounding title might be, apart
from its bearer's name, it is the trivializing sonority of Waugh's own
chiming prose that has performed in advance the satiric devaluation
of all such hierarchy and its heraldry.

And it has done so through a sustained reliance on disdainful
adjectival modification keyed to a snarky alliterative lilt. A syntax of plenitude in Woolf, of indulgent and dismissive repletion in
Waugh. A parallel grammar of itemization can as soon amass the
vitalizing urban facets of diurnal value as it can, in stultified form,
lambaste an entire registry of privilege in Waugh – and from opposite ends of a modernist aesthetic gamut, lyric reverie versus social
satire. In this sense, such a grammatical feature is certainly not
alone among the stylistic devices whose tone and mode, whose rhetorical suasion, can only be decided in situ – including, of course,

the considered and decisive adjective ("leaden," "uncouth"), alone or in consort.

And beyond the eccentricities of certain writers at opposite poles of their own stylistic epoch, a broader point should be stressed about a sense of such literary "moments" over literary-historical duration. Indeed, the following two subsections can refer, in their respective emphasis on modification and compounding, both to such grammatical aspects of a given sentence and to the cumulative changes in the time-sensitive features of such verbal modes over the continually *modified* course of literary-historical development – with its *compounded* backlog from author to author. With various devices now privileged, now adjusted, now scuttled, what grows apparent again is the way signature elements can define the tendencies of a period as well as the idiolect of a single author.

MODIFYING ELEMENTS (OVER SYNTAX AND TIME)

Predication is the backbone of writing, and modification inextricable from it – just as the syntactic tendencies of both are modified over time by currents of linguistic history and literary influence. In this long view, style can make strange bedfellows across genres, periods, modes, and narrative moods. One writer may seem appropriating and modifying the usages and habits of another by even the most circuitous of routes. Our concern, however, has been more often directed at the syntactic permutations in their own right. While keeping in mind the evolution of various rhetorical habits and tolerances, we will continue to track the byways of *style* per se, its effects and their fallout, across very different *styles* (in the recognizable authorial sense). Inverted phrasing can do one thing in Fielding and quite another in Melville – without us wanting to give up on recognizing the grammatical common denominators. Same with the echoic diction of "gloom." The value of style, after all, is that it funds diversity in the construction of phrases and clauses. Even some distinctive rhetorical effects, like chiasm or syllepsis, can operate quite differently in different narrative hands.

Take the consonant bracket we saw in Wharton, where the two-syllable noun "terror" is telescoped under pressure to release a whole inset lexeme. Even as the phonic bond of "terror tore" serves as a syncopated jolt to the compound "loneliness and terror" at Lily Bart's death, the displaced verbal emphasis seems in its own disruption to pinpoint the node of dread. Other phrasal displacements can capture different fates, mental states, and narrative velocities. After a threefold repetition of "settled" describing sheets of dust as they blanket the land in the Dust Bowl apocalypse that opens John Steinbeck's *The Grapes of Wrath* (1939), midway through the plot we hear of desperate California-bound itinerants, uprooted from their sharecropping and shelters, who "drove on to the West, flying from the road, flying from movement." The sentence turns upon two different senses of "from" (directional and causal: lifting off from driven hope and the road itself) – as if passionate speed could outstrip means en route to its destination.[5] Overt repetition now races ahead of itself as well, and this in another phonetic bracket (looser than Wharton's) that unpacks – by way of foreshadowed migrant idiom – an interim effect to its own cause and goal. For, in another cumulative sentence, "these lusted so greatly to be *settled* that they *set* their faces into the West and drove toward it, forcing the clashing engines over the roads" (196). Though the Midwest expatriates are not yet identified as *settlers* themselves, the urge to arrive as such injects the past participle of aspiration (and the only modifier they yearn for, "settled") with the vector of will it requires, carried forward into the doubled participial and adjectival syntax ("forcing"/"clashing") of an on-go-*ing* cumulative form, its kinetic rush anything but stabilized. Stressed in this way is the set purpose behind all such relocation, captured by an initial displacement phrasal as well as geographic. Such is the *drive* of Steinbeck's prose that the phonetic bracket of "settled" has thus set loose – or, more to the point, loosed "set" as – a lexical as well as social trajectory. Style has once again mapped plot.

Distinctive effects, I repeat, can operate quite differently in different hands. Take, for another example, the tendency toward adjectival congestion, for want of a better term: the pile-up (or chain link) of unpunctuated modifiers. Description can in this way perform its

own sense of the remorseless, the inevitably interlinked, the inseparable. And when modifiers pile up, they may sometimes be seen to
line up as well – and stretch out. In such usages they feel aptly bonded,
forming a nexus of equal players rather than a hierarchy of emphasis.
In either fashion, in crowding or elongation, they may appear work-
ing to inscribe, at the syntactic level, some linguistic "figure" of the
depicted. In the matter of accreted modifiers, the norm, of course,
involves a comma after each "nonrestrictive" adjective, except when
one seems to modify the next in line (almost adverbially) rather
than attach forward to the coming noun. A "chill, gloomy, dark grey
evening" is thus subtly different, in phrasing at least, from a "chill,
gloomy, grey, dark evening." No style involved, perhaps, but a difference: that's the only point so far. Remove such commas altogether,
though, in the service of a more deliberate stylistic effect, and something unexpected may seem extruded from their serial collision:
some extra quotient of jam-up in the oppressive thickening of gloom.
Dickens is the original master of this, in a spirited tendency only
gradually perfected in his novels; William Faulkner, the bearer of an
inheritance that, so far from being squandered in mere homage and
repetition, is reinvested at compound (and sometimes almost con-
founding) interest, in a key more often neurotic than comic. Dickens
and Faulkner: strange bedfellows indeed, and certainly no less when
asked to room with Thomas Pynchon or Cormac McCarthy or David
Foster Wallace or Don De Lillo. But just a few examples will show
how – and to what different ends – the first two writers, adduced here
in anticipation of their legacy, suspend the logic of restrictive modification for a simultaneous saturation of attributes, in everything from
comic recoil to the impression of mental duress.

By mid-career, Dickens has sophisticated the volatile effect
of his adjective chains so that unpunctuated compression may well
push both ways from a shifting center of gravity. In *Little Dorrit*, we
first meet Mr. Nandy as "a poor little reedy piping old gentleman, like
a worn-out bird."[6] This is a sequence in which "reedy" is tethered to
"little" in the column of ascribed frailness before it is nudged further
along to evoke the thin instrumental whine of a wind instrument:
that attenuated piping tweet of a spent bird in its futile chirps, caught

up in prose's own deliberate sing-song of sound and rhythm. Such mimic doubling is in full swing by the time of Dickens's last completed novel. Early, in a stunning anamorphic modification, there's the dowager Lady Tippins boasting "an immense obtuse drab oblong face, like a face in a tablespoon"[7] – where swelling and obtuseness are all there by rhythm alone in the oblong phrasing. And later in the novel, a waterside pub is described with a trio of unpunctuated adjectives rounded out by a separated fourth – then followed by two more plosive pressure points after the anchoring noun: "a narrow lopsided wooden jumble of corpulent windows heaped one upon another" (67)

Also approaching what we might call a hieroglyphic syntax, picturing in epithetical rhythm what its diction indicates to the eye, are the swifter adjectival prolongations of the earlier novel, *Great Expectations*. In the opening description, a flourish of low-keyed alliteration helps to delineate (and, in its own way, level) the uninflected horizon. Here is Woolf's "leaden" in linear rather than circular terms. Out of the mist and gloom in Dickens, the "low leaden line"[8] of the river stands forth as part of a marked line of prose, the effect being only enhanced with further adjectival distention. As darkness gathers, the "marshes were just a long black horizontal line": a lineation equally the work of typography in a quite different key – even without the "lead" type called up, perhaps, by that earlier adjective.

This unpunctuated format is relished in certain denigratory comic instances across all of Dickens's later novels, and not least in *Great Expectations*, where, lumberingly, there is Pumblechook: "a large hard-breathing middle-aged slow man." After the stressed syllabic assonance of "large" crowded by "hard," such symmetry is immediately dropped for that counterplay of quite different hyphenates. Among these, "slow" could have been slipped in anywhere, but seems appended here to emphasize not so much a laboriousness of person as this humbug's laggard pace of mind. Commas would certainly have divided his attributes misleadingly, since his ponderousness is all-consuming. Suffice it to say that, in Dickens, the pre-nominal adjectival pile-ups are rarely honorific. They are usually just what they seem: a satiric "dumping-on" the character or entity in question with a given set of traits, not aggrandizing such features in their repletion but trivializing them in the rut of undifferentiated mention, their negative facets all of a stylistically coerced piece. In this common effect of leveling or retardation – and whether the emphasis is pictorial or temporal – the thickening descriptors can take hold even when the effect is only marginally suggestive of some larger irony or disquiet. Nothing is propitious in Pip's "ascent" to London, including the tardy – and incidentally shabby – progress of his coachman in departure: "His getting on his box, which I remember to have been decorated with *an old weather-stained pea-green hammercloth moth-eaten* into rags, was quite a work of time." Here the first paired hyphenates seem orderly enough, logically sorted, in their move from a descriptive, past-participial modification ("weather-stained") to a strictly adjectival one ("pea-green") – until the rhyme-linked "m*oth*-eaten" (chiastic afterthought of "hammercl*oth*") brings with it again a sense of longstanding wear: all of this accreting syntax being a considerable work of grammatical duration in its own right. Just as a stretched-thin and unpunctuated prose line can seem to mirror a flattened landscape, sometimes writing can take the time it so differently depicts.

Mimetic syntax is quite variously installed in such Dickensian cases, whereas its equivalent in Faulkner, as we'll see, being dependent on a comparable adjectival fixation, is more likely to reflect a quality of obsession in the mode of perception itself, rather than any intrinsic qualities of the perceived object. In the later writer, the rhetorical effect of such adjectival traffic is typically found probing the ineffable in multiple attempts. Yet one generalization survives the historical and tonal difference between Victorian comedy or melodrama and Faulkner's southern gothic. Whether a variable descriptive nexus in Dickens or the symptom of a more overt psychological shackling in Faulkner, adjectival chains often tell a whole compressed story in its present traces. They emerge in this way as rhetorical microplots in their own right. This is overtly the case, certainly, in the haunted present of Faulkner's monomaniacal psychic atmospheres and their objective correlatives in ambient space, into which we'll be moving in a moment.

But the effect has other, quite different manifestations as well. Between Dickens and Faulkner, between the flamboyance of comedic phrasing and the obsessions of melodrama, one can locate a unique American vernacular on this stylistic gamut of such adjectival agglomeration. Syntactic figuration, in this case, can be no less effective when actually ungrammatical. In Mark Twain's *Adventures of Huckleberry Finn* (1884), adjectival congestion is often equivocated with adverbial use in Huck's semi-literate idioms, as when his recoil from the up-tight regimen of the Widow Douglas is immediate and instinctual, "considering how *dismal regular and decent* the widow was in all her ways"[9] – three adjectives or two (in the latter case with the implied adverb "dismally"), it hardly matters. And when the "sivilizing" imposition sets in again in the last chapter, Huck minces no words: "I can't stand it. I been there before" (220), where the lack of a proper grammatical past tense only suggests the eternal return of this threat.

In Faulkner's entrapping southern melodrama rather than Twain's unquenched picaresque, adjectives pile up, like everything else, with an ominous internal pressure striving for direction but often stalled in the mire of their own attribution. Take the opening of *Absalom, Absalom!* (1936): "From a little after two oclock until almost sundown of *the long still hot weary dead September afternoon* they sat," shuttered in a *"dim hot airless* room"[10] – the last a phrase with no breathing-room of its own. The contradictory double personification of the afternoon as both "weary" and "dead" meets a hairsbreadth of normalization in the way the hint of "dreary," as an impersonal modifier, is slipped halfway through the cracks at "hot weary." The explicit cracks are in the closed blinds, so that the room gradually "became *latticed* with yellow sl*ashes*" (7), prose itself patterned by an assonance slicing through the slats of phrasing in the faintest miming of intermittence. These penetrating gashes of light are "full of dust motes" whose pulverized monosyllabic forms "Quentin thought of as being flecks of the *dead old dried paint* itself blown inward from the scaling blinds." Right from the start of this novel, such Faulknerian adjectival chains are re-sorted into strange and unnerving covert hierarchies according to the slippages of double grammar. In the broached temporal spectrum of the opening phrase, "long still" suggests silent torpor until "still" shifts – or skids – ahead either as a separate epithet or a modifier of "hot": a heat lingering (still) despite the late hour. That's the modifier slumped forward, one might say, in this prolonged oppressive day: the adjective turned adverbial. But as the descriptive vise tightens in "still hot weary dead September afternoon," the modifiers also enfold each other in uncertain phrasal bunchings, so that the "weary" can either precede what amounts to a metaphoric repetition of stillness in "dead" or it can insinuate a reverse buckling with "still" for the idiomatic dead metaphor of "dead still" – hovering in abeyance as an unsaid cliché.

Primed by the relentless sound of such compression, it is just here that we encounter, from out of the darkening heat, "that grim haggard amazed" – and entirely personified – "*voice* of Miss Coldfield," a voice borrowing its decrepitude from her own bodily attributions in a triad of modification that makes "haggard" take on the aura of a past participle in itself, like the abutting "amazed." Further, the microplot thickens headily when we hear that the voice drones on "until at last listening would renege" – a refusal, that is, of anything like the hypertuned listening one brings to this sentence in hearing the split-second falling off from "last" to "list." The impasse comes, to complete the grammar in all its *and*-compounded fallout, when "listening would renege *and* hearing-sense self-confound" (8) – a remarkably awkward con-founding of predication in an unraveling grammar – "*and* the long-dead object of her impotent yet indomitable frustration would appear, as though by outraged recapitulation evoked, quite inattentive *and* harmless, out of the biding *and* dreamy *and* victorious dust" (8). In that spectral manifestation, the fivefold *and*-grammar, a parataxis of phrases and clauses alike, topples one wording into the next with a strange contradictory mix of panic and abandon, repression and release.

With not yet one full paragraph behind us in negotiating this Faulknerian prose, already attribution and retribution are inseparable in a writing studiously counter-intuitive – as well as backward-angled, hazed by precedent, retroactive, clotted by hauntings. In the inverted "as though by outraged recapitulation evoked" (8), the past participle has barely any semantic weight, the sense of emergence being already implicit. No semantic charge, that is, but still a certain mimetic force in its ornate rhetoric, almost meta-stylistic: an inversion as mannered and dated and stuck-in-the-past as is its human agency. On the heels of which, no sooner does "the biding" suggest a phonetic elision of "the abiding" than the prose decompresses, instead, along its *and*-grooved ground, augmenting beat by beat this figured manifestation of blocked desire. Via the rhetoric of compounding in this case, prose is synced with the dysfunctional time of regression, obsession, stagnation. So furiously obscure is the rhetoric in this claustrophobic passage that the echoic synesthesia in the "*loud cloud*y flutter of the sparrows" (8), audible from beyond the present claustrophobic enclave, offers a double epithet that could almost be taken to characterize the vacillating hazy syntactic bombast of Faulkner's own demands on the reading ear. No comma between "loud" and "cloudy," nor in "still hot weary dead September afternoon," nor in the otherwise serial "biding and dreamy and victorious dust." Thus has Faulkner spectralized, and elsewhere gothicized, and everywhere made mannerist, his legacy from the mimetic distentions or kaleidoscopic logjams of Dickensian modification, whose rebooting for such different narrative purposes makes the habit seem more dated yet in its cadences, fabled, inherited, in itself doomed to repetition.

Effects of this antiquating sort later in American literary history, building at times on Faulkner, are even more pronounced in the period style concocted by Thomas Pynchon for *Mason & Dixon* (1997), achieved sometimes by overt **archaism**, sometimes by a formality of diction and grammar less summarily outmoded – but redolent, nonetheless, of past rhetorical methods. "Once ashore," we read – with a shift from a quiet triadic assonance to a quite assertive tripling by way of an **elliptical** and inverted anaphora, "the Astronomers hear the Ocean everywhere, no Wall thick, nor Mind compos'd, nor valley remote enough, to lose it."[11] This is what a latter-day Milton might sound like if pastiching an eighteenth-century discursive pattern into a contemporary novel. But there is still room in such dat'd Prose for the more dramatic ramp-up of epithets Pynchon might have remembered in Faulkner, as in Mason's dream near the end, where again the pressure of assonance seems to trigger another order of accumulation, vertical in its mirage-like accretion as a looming monument. "Mason struggles to wake. He arises, glides to the Door," with the prose, at least, still in oneiric territory when he is stunned (by fourfold adjectival pile-up) "to find ascending before him one single dark extended Petroglyph."

Whatever overtones of Faulkner one might audit here, the influence is more obvious yet in another contemporary writer whose stylistic ambience of "savage quiet" would describe not the brooding silence of ferocious psychological repression, as in Faulkner, but the lulls between outright murderous atrocities of human predation. For it is in the ornate grammar and sonority of Cormac McCarthy's prose, in his historical pageants of carnage, that Faulkner's gothic has mutated into the genocidal grotesque. The overt landscapes of mayhem in McCarthy's prose tend to render the serene balance of chiastic inversion, for instance, and similar rhetorical flourishes, uniquely perverse in their uncanny symmetrical exertions – with the force of style operating as if in recoil, stunned rather than purgative, from its assigned subject matter of unstinted brutality.

COMPOUNDED FORM (FROM AUTHOR TO AUTHOR)

If the pneumatic pressure built up by piled adjectival inevitability in Faulkner is the functional complement of his *and*-strings – one impression sedimenting another through an inexorable dovetailed form – then the melodramatics of either form of compounding, conjunctive or adjectival, can be borrowed separately for comparable effects. McCarthy gravitates to the *and*-grammar for a kind of unedited sense of narratival momentum, except when saturating action with the florid rhetoric associated with its historical settings. Punctuation comes and goes, but the sense of enchained consequences always carries the whiff of the inevitable, even in the simplest cases. Here, for example, is compound grammar at work in *Blood Meridian* (1985) in a way that involves the most straightforward sense of delay and acceleration, halt and renewed impetus, as pivoted on two lackluster senses of "call" in its variant idiomatic use: "The captain called a halt and he called up the Mexican who served as guide. They talked and the Mexican gestured and the captain gestured and after a while they moved on again."[12] The bland consecutivity of such parataxis, with unpunctuated clausal compounding, can generate a very different tone in more labored and ominous passages, as here in a bounty-hunting gang's retreat from the brutal massacre of an Indian encampment: "They were riding in pure sand and the horses labored so hugely that the men were obliged to dismount and lead them, toiling up steep eskers where the wind blew the white pumice from the crests like the spume from sea swells" (175). More arresting than the simile itself, perhaps, is the almost anagrammatic eye/ear (mis)match of "pumice" with "spume." And more is coming, pasted in by further compounds: "*and* the sand was scalloped *and* fraily shaped *and* nothing else was there save random polished bones" (175). Spatial progress is all but sunk in an overload, or quicksand, of "random" additive impressions. Yet it is important to recognize how the grammatical engineering of such contingent and unsorted compounding, prey to any stray notice, can operate not just as a residual vigilance in a world of violent surprise but as a mode of the pastoral uncanny in a text from the same century to which *Blood Meridian* casts back, here a moment of picaresque interruption in no less an American landmark than *Huck Finn*, its freeform cascade of association by no means spoiled by punctuation:

The stars were shining, *and* the leaves rustled in the woods
ever so mournful; *and* I heard an owl, away off, who-whooing
about somebody that was dead, *and* a whippowill *and* a dog crying
about somebody that was going to die; *and* the wind was trying to
whisper something to me, *and* I couldn't make out what it was, *and*
so it made the cold shivers run over me (3).

Amid the freefall of causality in the text's self-conscious half-literacy, the very sound of the onomatopoetic "who-ing" owl seems to comment stylistically on the inappropriate "that" grammar for a person, even if only a corpse. The unprocessed lyric gloom of this interlude, fused loosely by conjunctions, displays some of the same unsorted sensorium of natural impressions orchestrated by McCarthy's prose, where, in the passage just quoted, style opens itself to the bombardment of landscape's duress, or elsewhere its discrepant splendor, between episodes of executed carnage.

It is in fact the plot's most recent and perhaps most egregious bloodshed that those laboring horsemen have just left behind in *Blood Meridian*. As anticipated from the novel's euphonious subtitle forward, *Or the Evening Redness in the West*, its prose gravitates to the purple at its most intense and wrenching – or at least to a bruised crimson. No living writer has more obvious rhetorical power at his brandished command than McCarthy. Call it overkill in the evocation of mayhem or not, it is obvious that words get in the way of unmediated revulsion, even while revving it up. The balancing act is extraordinary, and not unlike the compensatory stylistic ecstasy deployed earlier in Nabokov's *Lolita* to convert illicit sexual obsession, and its actual human violations, into an impersonal stratosphere of aesthetic delirium. These two very different authors, Nabokov and McCarthy – strange bedfellows again – meet recently, a chapter apart, in a book by Lee Clark Mitchell with the polemic title *Mere Reading*, which suggests not the indifference of passive consumption but the isolated attention to writing's own fashioning work in an academic climate of more ideological investments.[13]

Nabokov is, in fact, capable of a violent image almost as repugnant as one of McCarthy's in the latter's scrutinized onslaughts of rape, pillage, and dismemberment. Quaint breakfast-table diction and a bouncy alliteration numbs Humbert, the narrator of *Lolita*, but not us, to his unloved wife's body after a car accident, "the top of her head a porridge of bone, brains, bronze hair and blood."[14] And Faulkner comes to mind, though not his fevered solemnities, in erotic passages of compulsive desire, here with an overdone alliterative compounding of the transferred epithet (moral displaced to physical attribute) in the hissed friction of Lolita's "shameless innocent shanks" (60), elsewhere her "guileless limbs" (58), the latter a favored noun under various adjectival pressure and phonetic caress, as in "four limpid lovely limbs" (192). Highlighting the sound quotient of the narrator's outpoured lust, he even composes a "madrigal" to, among other charms, the half musical, half graphic chiasm entailed by the "*blond down* of her *brown limbs*" (44) – those ultimate "nymphet's limbs" (257) that tempt the mental tongue with a spasm of false anticipation: in precisely that non-plosive *p* in phantom foreplay en route to the muted puckered *b*.

Although these particular instances are not called out in Mitchell's extensive subsection on "Stylistic Evasions, and Oscillations" in *Lolita*, they bear a queasy relation to his later citation from one of the more gruesome passages in McCarthy, a tour de force of phantasmagoric violence whose bloody traces, the narrator remarks, will leave no enduring historical mark. Mitchell notes the self-correcting irony whereby the passage itself bears hideous witness to the deed, a writing that "etches its memory for later generations" (185). He thus stresses what Altieri might call a "valuation" of the passage when "style transfigures the scene," most notably, "in the oddly lush simile" (186) that confronts us – in just the episode that precedes the horsemen's difficult trek past this scene of their slaughter, quoted above – with "skulls like polyps bluely wet or luminescent melons cooling on some mesa of the moon" (McCarthy, 174). Style's attempted value could hardly be clearer: "Violence receding in time paradoxically endures for posterity in the scene's phrasing itself" (186). Mitchell adduces this as a case in point for his eponymous restorative project of "mere reading," aligned by him with a broader neoformalist emphasis on surface articulation. Yet in its nuanced and considered attention to just what is before us, an attention slow and scarcely superficial, he might have, with less modesty, called it *sheer reading* instead.

And the ghoulish peculiarity of that "oddly lush simile" can be even more slowly "evaluated" (this, again, in Barthes's subdividing and typological sense from the Introduction). Phrasing is enhanced by perverse euphony in the sound play accompanying those peeled craniums, from *pol* through *blu* to *lu*, the *lumin* then shuffled to *melon*, before the internal rhyme of *cooling* with *moon*. It is as if an avoided truism is buried by the orotund: such horror is indeed *other worldly* – as if extraterrestrial, if not dredged from undersea ("polyps"). Yet not emotionally distanced thereby. There is no laziness in letting readers choose their preferred simile, for neither serves for a minute, still less the two together, to buffer the nauseating scene. The either/or is a rare move in the style of literary similitude. We've seen it before only in the "burlesque" analogizing of Fielding's *Joseph Andrews*, where Slipslop, as yet unnamed, is, in her lust, figured as both terrestrial lioness and underwater predator. The effect there was farcical: worth remembering – in order to see how closely McCarthy skirts here, from the midst of a genocidal gothic, the rhetorical tone of black comedy. Yet the unimaginable violence remains un-imageable, for all the metaphors that have built up around it, including even the phonemic mimesis of a hideously round (and all but palindromic) "polyp" in its macabre latent association with flesh turned to flayed "pulp."

So-called *graphic* violence is rendered so pictorially lavish, here and everywhere in McCarthy, that the dividing line between loveliness and repugnance in wording, even under erosion, is all the more clearly marked – and reinforced. And about all the nonwords to follow historically in this recovered scene of the forgotten, we hear further, along another *and*-terraced unpunctuated plummet into the inevitable, that "in the days to come the frail black rebuses of blood in those sands would crack *and* break *and* drift away so that in the circuit of few suns all trace of the destruction of these people would be erased." Conjunctive grammar is the least of it, however, in this irreversible course of erasure, where corrosive saline gusts are played off, as follows, against a more normative phrase like *salt their wounds*: "The desert wind would salt their ruins and there would be nothing, nor ghost nor scribe, to tell to any pilgrim in his passing how it was that people had lived in this place and in this place died" (*BM*174). The burnished archaism of "nor ghost nor scribe" again registers such prose as itself quasi-historical, even in this denial of scribal record. Equally dated, classical, almost biblical, and thus equally serving to lift this snapshot of monstrous brutality into the cadences of epic testimony, is the ambivalent grammar of the final chiasm. By its torqued logic, the landscape is its own failed narrative, not just record, with nothing "to tell ... how it was that people had lived in this place" – "how it was" meaning both the fact that it was

and *in what manner*: a double sense both receding and yet unforgiv-
ingly present in the syntactic reversal of the finishing phrase, "and in
this place died." That they lived and died is the anthropological fact;
how it was that they died is the further political tale to "tell," conveyed in all its ineffable negative affect by similitudes phonetic and
figurative alike, none alone capable of the dark charge it has assumed.

Stylistic "oscillations" (Mitchell's term) are certainly on offer
in a very different novel of the next decade, in the mode of skeptical
carnivalesque rather than apocalyptic furor. David Foster Wallace is
a scruffy mercurial stylist who segues into vernacular monologues
that can at times seem designed almost to transliterate Joycean
polylingualism and syllabic dismemberment – what Joyce called the
"phonemanon"[15] – into semi-literate rant. One comes to suspect that
the *Infinite Jest* of Wallace's most famous title suggests in part the
unstoppable punning of words in "trancemission" (a self-exampling
case, 129). With overtones of Slipslop's malapropisms in Fielding two
and a half centuries back, on the same page *eliminate* comes through
as "elomonade." There, too, an Asian racial slur actually slurs the
verbal report of a pilfered bookbag in its run of three noun modifiers,
the bag stolen "off a foran slop studn type kid," where the slack third
adjectivalized spelling is completed by the first sound of the next
idiomatic noun modifier in "studen(t) type kid."

As often happens in closure, even in a novel as willfully open-
ended as Wallace's, many earmarked stylistic effects are brought to
bear. Not just the buildup of adjectives has its precedent in Faulkner,
but so does Wallace's fondness, like Cormac McCarthy's, for the lax
latchings of unpunctuated *and*-compounds. In the last episode before
the final drug orgy at the novel's nonfinite end, a character named
Orin is trapped in a vast "bathroom-type tumbler" (971), accosted
through the glass with a (lexically self-amplified) "stilted amplified
voice" whose double modification spins almost out of control when
characterized further as making "the sort of *surreal disorienting
nightmarish incomprehensible but vehement* demand that often gets
made in really bad dreams" (972). This undifferentiated splay of quali-
fication is a fine Faulknerian match to the unprioritized *and*-rendered
grammar of the nightmare's preceding description, with no commas

to weigh, rank, or pace the processed impression, including its embedded adjectival jam: "Its glass was green *and* its bottom over his head was pebbled *and* the light inside was the *watery dancing* green of extreme ocean depths" (971). The Faulknerian overtones of all this are not left entirely to our inductive inference. We are given, instead, one meta-allusion – in the form of in-joke – to secure our literary historical recognition. For the narrative conjures Faulkner explicitly at one point in a stylistic rear-view mirror of inertial modification. The occasion is the recorded confidence that sex between parents, as imagined by their children, is always likely to be "frenetic and weary, with a kind of doomed timeless Faulknerian feel to it" (957).

Later, in the drug delirium of the novel's last paragraph, the first instance of mimetic adjectival crowding – here almost literal compaction – occurs in the sentence fragment "Strong squat hard kid" (as contrasted, for instance, with "the bland groomed corporate guy" earlier in the chapter [976]). Such an accordion-squeeze of modification (and phonetic compression as well) in "stro*ng s*quat *ha*rd" is then answered, just before the protagonist's passing out, when the "last thing Gately saw" was himself in a mirroring mirage. In the last phase of an unpunctuated continuum, "he looked into the square *and* saw clearly a reflection of his *own big square pale* head with its eyes closing as the floor finally pounced." One more sentence sees the novel out by bringing Gately back to consciousness, but not to the hallucinatory room he had previously occupied: "And when he came back to," – rather than just "came to," as if to anticipate the spatial return that is instead deflected – "he was flat on his back ... " A standard series is next spaced out (colloquial sense too) by an extra conjunction (as if seeped through from beach "s*and*") – though this time with commas serving to demarcate the stages and foci of returned perception. Amid a spate of awkwardly re-orienting prepositions, the main clause of restored cognition finds him "flat *on* his back *on* the beach *in* the freezing sand, *and* it was raining *out of* a low sky, *and* the tide was *way out*" (796). Way far out. After all the addled frenetic free indirect discourse of the blinding drug high, confronted with this last moment of focalized recognition, – can we force ourselves to rule out an idiom just because of its unsaid status?

Aren't we well within the orbit here, the gesture and the jest, of the stoner argot "far out"?

Wallace certainly has his own nervous, manic way with the *and*-juggernaut, even in its tailed-off versions. Elsewhere – and whether in regard to "compoundings" between phrases or, by phonetic accretion, within and across their internal wording – the Faulknerian tradition persists, even if mostly another name for a stylistic baroque in postwar American fiction. Yet precisely in its stylistic manifestation, Faulkner's racial thematic has a more obvious lineage as well. In the line of African-American prose that has borrowed so much from the phrasal bravura of Faulkner's syntactic gothic, the language of Ralph Ellison's *Invisible Man* (1952) is repeatedly heated into an implied stylistic "valuation" of its racialized perceptions. As a young black man transfixed by the nude dancing of a blonde girl behind "veils" of the gawkers' smoke in an early chapter, for instance, the eponymous hero responds to the performer's total visibility – in something of the style of a Joycean "epiphany" – with a throat-tightening run of guttural phonemes in spillover from a quasi-anagrammatic phrasal span: "She seemed like a fair *bird-girl girdled* in veils calling to me from the an*gry* surface of some *gray* and threatening sea. I was transported."[16] The "transport" – into a "gray" place neither black nor white – is confirmed by the dizzy momentum of the prose alone, in both its far-flung nautical trope and its internal syllabic figuration. Just as "angry" will eventually release "gray" by syllabic expansion, so have the incremental contortions of *ird-girl-girdld* served in their own right – as in a separate bump-and-grind of lexical sequence – to reiterate another vowel-consonant nucleus within the mimetic girdling of a phonetic bracket. Responding to "pressing" urges internal to wording (as expressed most explicitly by Don DeLillo in this chapter's next and closing section), style emerges here in Ellison as writing's own furious ("angry") libido.

No less so, one should add, in the work of Ellison's successor, Toni Morrison, whose ear has learned as much from his phrasal intensity as from Faulkner's. And this despite the potentially misleading statement in the "Foreword" to *Beloved*: "To render enslavement as a personal experience, language must get out of the way."[17]

This is more than a question of ineffable – unsayable – suffering. For characters in the plot, searing memories take embodied rather than phrased form. Yet, by a deep literary irony, only style can convey this degree of the unspeakable. Sustained cruelty has, we hear in retrospect, "punched the glitt*ering iron*" (with its implacable silent clang) "out of Sethe's eyes, leaving two open wells" – left as if across the gape of its own caesura – "that did not reflect firelight" (11). She lives on within a more ominous optical aura. On Paul D's return to Sethe's haunted world, after further grief and death amassed and summarized in the backstory of this first chapter, the "iron was back," but firelight has been replaced by the afterglow of violence, whose own implied "wells" are unstaunched as we watch him "step inside her door smack into a pool of pulsing red light" (11). The slight jolt of syntactic interruption across the broken verb phrase "step smack into" lends further emphasis to the capillary syllabic lapping at "p*ool* of *pul*sing" in its blood-red diffusion – this, before the image is normalized to the idiomatic dead metaphor of "waves of grief" in the next paragraph. "Language," in the sense of historical or polemical discourse, may have gotten "out of the way" in such a figured personalization of enslaved life, but style is left to carry the rhetorical burden into words.

PRESSING MEANING: A PHONETIC RETROSPECT

Just over half a decade after the American disaster of 9/11, the twin towers are exploded and toppled again in Don De Lillo's 2007 *Falling Man*. Stylistic "valuation" would be unavoidable, even if we didn't know, from a notable interview, how much such effects were explicitly on the novelist's, this novelist's, mind in all his work. After the hijacked planes bring down the towers: "The light drained dead away, bright day gone."[18] The wording is like an overcrowded, phonetically imploded metrical passage out of Tennyson, the echo of "light" with "bright" in counterpoint with the contraction of "drain(e)d dead" – sluiced away into the metonymically lost "day" of occluded daylight. "The only light was vestigial now, the light of what comes after, carried in the residue of s*mashed mat*ter" (246) – where apposition then pulverizes the very epithet in restatement. For what ensues reads as if "ash" were there at the unavoidable core of the collapse: a smashing crash manifested "in ash ruins of what was various and human, hovering in the air above" (246). Even before the faintly chiastic switch form "hov/er" to "air … ove," what we are left with, in phonetic as well as ocular residue, is what might be thought to constitute, beyond the simple bracketing assonance of "ruin" against "human," a trans-word anagram (graphic and aural alike) of the same "ruin" dispersed, disintegrated, across "va*rious* and h*uman*."

Graphic and aural alike: audiovisual. DeLillo's revealing 1993 interview in the *Paris Review* puts none of this past the likelihood of his intention, let alone his seasoned resources. Perhaps nowhere in the annals of English fictional writing do we have a writer's sense of style so clearly wedded to sentence form and its aural engineering. Whatever else DeLillo is engaged upon in drafting his fictions, "the basic work is built around the sentence. This is what I mean when I call myself a writer. I construct sentences."[19] And what is the temporal infrastructure of that construction? "There's a rhythm I hear that drives me through a sentence. And the words typed on the white page have a sculptural quality. They form odd correspondences. They match up not just through meaning but through sound and look." Such is his prose poetics, and, as such, a matter of syllabic beat – and its sonic (i.e., phonic) constituents. "The rhythm of a sentence will accommodate a certain number of syllables. One syllable too many, I look for another word. There's always another word that means nearly the same thing, and if it doesn't then I'll consider altering the meaning of a sentence to keep the rhythm, the syllable beat." In Jacobson's terms from our Introduction, rhyme wins out over discursive reason, the paradigmatic axis over the syntagmatic, echoic equivalence over strict combinatory syntax. "I'm completely willing to let language press meaning upon me." And thus push the sentence along. DeLillo's is not an ex-pressive aesthetic in any ordinary sense, but a propulsive one. On this understanding of fiction writing, wording is in the driver's seat; style is the result; any narrative microplot must shift its synchromeshed gears to accommodate.

And this approach to language's internal compulsions is even more specifically lexical and phonetic than it may at first sound: "Watching the way in which words match up, keeping the balance in a sentence – these are sensuous pleasures. I might want *very* and *only* in the same sentence, spaced a particular way, exactly so far apart. I might want *rapture* matched with *danger* – I like to match word endings." And their onsets as well. Listen in this sense, as the twin towers fall to rubble, to the chiastic expansion – and mimetic collapse – of "h*eard*" into its nightmare grammatical object: not just as "*dru*mming," but as the self-echoing "*dru*mming *rum*ble" (246). Need one stress – so near the close of our sampling – the stylistic retrospect this affords? Who is disposed "to match word endings" (or, in a self-exampling double grammar, who likes matching word endings) – or beginnings, for that matter – more than Poe or Dickens? Who, describing a dreary "pair" of "mirrors" in a decaying house, would be eagerer than Dickens, for instance, to install their own dysllabic mirroring, even in British spelling, as a "pair of meag*re* mir*rors*"?[20] When critic John Mullan, in his chapter on "Style" in *How Novels Work*, highlighting the tendency toward parataxis in DeLillo's *Underworld* (1997), quotes a long *and*-chain grammar about rival pigeon-keepers releasing their flocks from New York rooftops, what the excerpt embeds, unmentioned, is something like a lower-order parataxis – a kind of syllabic enjambment, at the lexical rather than syntactic level – in the gnarled phonetics of "a hun*dred*-bir*ded* tum*ul*t and b*lur*."[21] In this novelist who leans toward cross-mated word endings, that syllabic anagram of hyphenated closing syllables is then answered by the subsequent phonemic chiasm of *ul/lu*. So it is that the paratactic grammar of run-on may find its scaled-down counterpart in syllabic overrun.

Suffice it to say, then, that in speaking up for the sounds of words as a motoring force in the sentence, as structuring unit of narrative, DeLillo is also speaking out, with unprecedented explicitness, for the phonic texture of literary prose all told, including that of his American forebears in Poe and Melville and Faulkner. Indeed, the effort of ekphrasis – the verbal representation of a visual object – throws DeLillo's phonetics into special relief. Listen to the narrator's looking at satellite overviews adjusted to translate geographic data into coded image, including the sibilant zing of "sizable cities pixeled into mountain folds."[22] In characterizing an enhanced topography, the sentences have their own, including the "*patches* of *lustrous color*" generated by "computer *fuschi*as or ror*schach* pulses of unnamed shades" (415). The pixelated "underworld" of the digitized image, in transfiguring landscape to photogenic data panels, has here found its objective correlative in the busy substrate of syntax itself, yielding up, a short paragraph later, "some hallucinatory fuse of exactitude and rapture" (415). It is as if the 1993 interview about the desired echo of closing syllables in the conjectural wedding of "rap*ture*" with "dan*ger*" has been recalled half a decade later for the subtler mix of precision and ecstasy in his prose's own "fuschia"-triggered "fuse" – and fusion – of a lexical, rather than pictographic, "exactitude and rapture."

The novel called *Underworld* brings itself to a halt by making unmistakable its title's allusion to cyberspace as unseen ground to all figuration in the contemporary system of global communication, verbal as well as visible. In a last sounding (both senses) of this eponymous spatial metaphor, the novel ends with the narrator's almost Zen-like concentration on the pixel-borne, monitor-framed image of a single word and its underlying cyber-searched etymology, as spelled out only in the last one-word paragraph. The end-stopped monosyllable "Peace." (827) puts a period to the novel even while it wavers there in page space between isolated diction and motivated valediction. Suspended between vessel of philology and colloquial exhortation, between ancient polylingual word form (*pax*, etc.) and imperative clause, this noun of quietude operates in gestalt flip with its verbal alter ego, surfaced by back-formation, in an elliptical predicate of address – as if to say "Peace be with you." Before the final citation of the anticipated "seraphic word" (the quasi-anagrammatic epithet itself containing all the letters of the quite different phonemic form p-e-a-c-e), its first manifestation is ether-eal in the technological sense, appearing "in the lunar milk of the data stream" (826). Maintaining the liquid status of the dead metaphor "stream," the figurative "lunar milk" catches the sense of a backlit translucent medium in which the word is floated into view, allowing the screen user – in this new fluidity of computer *literacy*, and in what one might call the title scene of the novel – to "follow the word through the tunneled underworld of its ancestral roots." Roots – and new branches, for it is "a word that spreads a longing through the *raw* sprawl of the city and out across the dreaming bourns and orchards to the solitary hills" (827). Where we began with Defoe's tactically heavy prepositions, here, in radical contrast, we have the thru-line of their diffusive music: *through / of / out / across / to.*

Contemporary prose is an apt place to summarize and look back, distilling what we've sampled from Defoe through Dickens to DeLillo. If a novel is a verbally incarnate world in motion, linguistic possibility has always been the "tunneled underworld" of its events, like the Ethernet netherworld in DeLillo's organizing mastertrope. As bodied forth in the pulse of chosen wording, language is fiction's underlying arterial lifeblood. And more technological tropes than this have been of use well before computerization. If books, as I. A. Richards famously put it in the late 1920s, are "machines to think with" – by way of, as well as along with – then style is their synaptic circuitry.[23] On that it is hard to, and impossible not to, *put a value.* Symptomatic reading after all: in diagnostic lingo, this is how representation *presents* on the page. The prose of fiction manifests the central nervous system of narrative writing – and of its thinking reception. Whether or not content takes direct dictation from form – to whatever extent meaning may be pressured, that is, by inner linguistic shaping as well as overall rhetorical intent – style remains nothing less than the materialization of idea in words.

5 Inventory
Some Terms of Engagement – A to Z

The fact that the following limited list, in reviewing only vocabulary risen to the occasion of given illustrations in the preceding chapters, offers a mix of categories – variously drawn from linguistics, phonetics, etymology, grammar, rhetoric, poetics, and narrative theory – is exactly the point about the amalgamating work of style.

Absolute Construction: a grammatical halfway house (derived from the Latin "ablative absolute") that is not quite freestanding as syntax, but is instead balanced independently between clause (full predication) and participial phrase (latched to a main sentence form or grammatical "kernel"), as in "pumps going in leaky ships" (Dickens); often part of the syntactical annex that builds a **cumulative** sentence

Adjective Chain: epithets piled up before (sometimes after) a noun without separate punctuation, a device frequent in Dickens ("a poor little reedy piping old gentleman") and turned melodramatic in James with "the wide overwhelming presence" and all but mannerist in Faulkner ("the long still hot weary dead September afternoon"); often involving a sequence of "restrictive" adjectives applying separately, one after the other, to the noun – rather than to another of its modifiers – and thus normally requiring the comma separation that is overridden by such a jammed or enchained effect

Alliteration: the opening of separate words with the same consonant or vowel sound, as in the satire of "*c*rumbling *c*ountry seats" (Waugh) – as immediately expanded into the comparable cross-stitched silliness of soundplay in "i*ll*iterate *l*airds from wet granite *h*ove*l*s in the *H*igh*l*ands"

Anagram: the shuffling of the same letters for another separate lexical unit, usually a whole word, either in graphic form (like *silent/listen*) or (less discussed) in phonetic form – and sometimes only as involved, in quasi-anagrammatic fashion, with internal syllabic matter rather than whole word units, as in "bir*d-girl girdl*ed" (Ellison), or shunted into the eye-only effect of short- against long-*u* sounds in "pumice"/"spume" (McCarthy)

Anaphora: metaphoric function ("likeness") in a strictly linguistic rather than figurative sense, forged by repetition at the beginning of sequential phrases or clauses, as in the fourfold case of "in and out" repeated as adverbial header in the nautical density of Thames traffic (Dickens) or the antiquing of prose in "no Wall thick, nor Mind compos'd, nor valley remote enough" (Pynchon)

Animism: see **Personification**

Apostrophe: a direct address, in the vocative case, to an absent or inanimate object, as ironized in the narrator's prolonged interrogation of Judge Pyncheon's corpse in Hawthorne

Appositive: verb phrase or noun phrase inserted or appended to restate another, as in "to burn always with this hard gemlike flame, to maintain this ecstasy" (Pater) or "life, London, this moment of June" (Woolf)

Archaism: dated and self-conscious literary vocabulary, as when Melville's narrator is made to sound like Milton, or as in the antiquated version of neither/nor in McCarthy's "nor ghost nor scribe"

Assonance: sonority in sequence, marked by the repetition of vowel sounds within successive (or narrowly separated) words (framed by alliterative effects, as well, in Dickens's "il*lum*ines the g*loom*" or Faulkner's "*la*tticed with yellow s*lashes*")

Back-formation: though sometimes made available for stylistic emphasis, a more basic philological process by which a noun emerges over etymological time from an initial verb form, or vice versa (in Scott, for example, "remains" as noun)

Chiasm: from the Greek *chi* for X, a "crossing" (in the general spirit of symmetry) arranged by clauses, phrases, syllables, or **phonemes** balanced against each other by a mirror reversal of structure, as when a parallelism like *abab* becomes instead the inverted or pivotal *abba* –

sensed minimally, at the syllabic level, for instance, in the switch from "dro*ll*ery" to "*l*ow" (Fielding)

Circumlocution: circling an idea with more words (more "locution") than strictly needed, as in the cognitive discovery of Biblical relevance in a strained emphasis like "felt *what kind* of sickness of the heart it *was which* arises from hope deferr'd" (Sterne) – or, often, in more comic ramblings

Compounding: the basic *and*-grammar of coordination, sometimes implemented as a piling up of unpunctuated items in nonserial form, as in the **paratactic** "out of the biding *and* dreamy *and* victorious dust" (Faulkner)

Cross-word play: a drift of syllabic (or, more often, subsyllabic) phonemes across spaced word gaps (breaching what linguists call the demarcations of "juncture"), so that wording no longer strictly respects lexical borders, as manifested in aural effects ranging everywhere from a mimetic density in "thick gloom" (Poe) to translexical puns "like arrow of light" (Conrad) or "full of" explicitly releasing "love" a few words further on (Forster); what, in a more technical linguistic analysis for *Reading Voices*, I termed "transegmental drift"

Cumulative sentence: a grammatical format in which a main (or kernel) clause is amplified by attached phrases, usually participial (and usually in *ing* rather than *ed* form), in a manner that spreads out action or description from the central moment referred to, as in Dickens when "among the tiers of shipping" is modified by a ripple effect of phrasing based on "avoid*ing* ... sink*ing* ... scatter*ing* ... cleav*ing*," etc., or in Steinbeck's "drove on to the West, fly*ing* from the road, fly*ing* from movement"

Dead metaphor: a word or phrase lapsed over time from figurative usage to mere idiomatic formulation, yet sometimes available for reanimation – as in George Eliot when "waves of her own sorrow" induce a "shipwreck"

Double entendre: from French "double intention" or "double hearing," a thus self-exemplified term for taking a word or phrase in two different senses, either grammatically distinguished, as in "to begin my life with the beginning of my life" (Dickens), or compacted into a single lexeme, as when "one with" does double duty for "won with" in the vicinity of "wondrous" (George Eliot)

Double grammar: William Empson's notable coinage for syntax that pulls two ways at once from center, as in the ambiguous attachment of the adverb *still* (spatial and temporal) in "farther back still seemed" (Conrad)

Ellipsis: the dropping out of unnecessary grammatical material that remains understood, often due to a parallelism of structure, as with the elliptical **fragments** of a mirror that remains the continuous implied subject of "Reflects the new Veneering crest ... Reflects Veneering ... Reflects Mrs. Veneering ..." (Dickens) or "Peace" taken as an imperative (for "Peace be with you") rather than a noun (DeLillo)

Epithet: an adjective, sometimes recursive or formulaic, that may be congregated with other such modifiers, punctuated or not (see **adjective chain**), or that may be illogically **transferred** to the object modified, as in "leaden circles" for the rippling of metallic bell sounds (Woolf) or "guileless limbs" (Nabokov)

Finite verb: a predication that establishes the tense of an action, whether transitive (taking an object in the accusative case) or intransitive (not), as opposed to the unmarked temporality of an infinitive

Fragmentation: the isolated (and technically ungrammatical) phrasing of either subject or predicate alone, not operating as part of a full syntactic unit – often understood by the logic of **ellipsis**

Free indirect discourse: the report on a character's thoughts or speech without quotation marks, absorbing personality or privacy into the discourse of omniscience, as in Austen's treatment of the wordy Mr. Collins when, given cordial treatment by a woman he has just met, he receives it as an act of deference that he (as the narrator ventriloquizes him) "could not help flattering himself, however, might be justified by his relationship to the young ladies who introduced him to her notice"

Fricative: for *v* sounds that have the effect of forced air, and are thus associated at times with a representational friction apart from the passage of breath against teeth and tongue that produces it – as in the whizzing "arrow of light" suggesting, by cross-word play, "of flight" (Conrad)

Genitive: the preposition *of*, indicating degrees of "possession" across a range of grammatical objects or conditions, whether subjective (the love *of her family* for travel), objective (her love *of family*), or equative (a family of [constituted by] the like-minded), the last equative form as found in Scott's "feeble voice of murmur" or in Wharton's "indistinct sense of drowsy peace" when sensation itself is the referent

Gerund: *ing* lexeme in substantive use, serving as a noun rather than a present-tense participle or modifier, as in Lawrence's equivocation for "the consummation of my *being* and of her *being*" (noun or participle or both) "in a new one"

Hendiadys: from the Greek for "one-via-a-duo," the use of a conjunction to divide up a phrase that would normally involve subordinate modification, as in Wilde's "swiftness and motion" instead of "swift motion"

Homophone: verbal material sounding like two different word forms at once, whole or in part, including the tacitly thematized play on Jane "ere now" (Brontë) or on "polysemous" as poly-seamed (Miéville)

Infinitive: the *to* form of the verb, before being relegated to any assigned finite tense – and sometimes played off against its prepositional double, as in "*to drive to* wherever it was I was supposed *to be*" (Ishiguro)

Intransitive: verb form indicating an action or motion or emotion taking no object, thus operating in a finite grammar of self-sufficiency, as in the first of the run-on clauses in "I went to sleep Henry Jekyll, I awakened Edward Hyde" (Stevenson)

Inversion: the flip of normal grammatical order in either clauses or phrases, as when a verb precedes its noun subject ("Sounded at last the bell," say) as well as in the front-loaded preposition of "Out it boomed" (Woolf) or the delayed past participle in "as though by outraged recapitulation evoked" (Faulkner)

Iterative tense: a verb form that indicates repeated, cyclic action or condition, with a sense of recurrence that Huck Finn's language can approximate by its own lapse in grammar, foundering between past and present when "I been there before," is meant to look back on the perpetual threat of civilizing influences (Twain)

Latinate (versus Germanic or Anglo-Saxon): the aura of lexical origin often associated with formal or official prose, as sometimes mismatched for stylistic effect with words of more native and vernacular derivation, as in the self-styled "burlesque diction" (Fielding) of his phrase "voracious pike"

Lexeme: word unit

Malapropism: wrong word choice, as when a character means "the lightest hint suffices" in saying the "lightest hint sophisticates" (Fielding) or "elemonade" for "eliminate" (Wallace)

Metalepsis: an intersection of author with character at a rhetorical level suddenly manifest in the story world, as if in a real-life encounter, as when a character is disturbed by his narrator's imaginary surveillance in Sterne: "As I darkened the little light he had, he lifted up a hopeless eye towards the door ..."

Metaphor: category of figurative language that replaces (or equates) one thing with its resemblance, as in "A Christmas frost had come at midsummer" for blighted hopes (Brontë)

Metonymy: a figure of speech (a subclass of metaphor) that substitutes an idea or object for another with which it is associated, as in "day gone" for "daylight gone" (DeLillo)

Microplot: a site-specific verbal form in which some broader inflection or tension of story is rehearsed, replayed, or condensed into phrasing's own grammatical action and rhetorical force, as in a distilled manner – across a syllabic echo of reciprocation verging on pun – in "Anne was tenderness itself, and she had the full *worth* of it in Captain Went*worth*'s affection" (Austen)

Mimetic phrasing (diction or syntax): as a concerted subset of "mimesis" (or representation) more generally, the sound (or sequence) of words that appears specifically shaped (or timed) to the event or scene being described – a kind of verbal mime, as in the back-loaded modification of "a hammer hovered backwardly uplifted" (Melville)

Narratography: a stylistic subset of narratology (the "science" of narrative) concerned (in my coinage) with the actual literary inscription of story in diction and syntax, rather than narrative's broader cognitive parameters in any medium

Onomatopoeia: a case of word sounds echoing referential sense, either in the formal contrivance of a given sentence or in lexemes identified in their own right as of "imitative" origin, such as "murmur" (Scott)

Oxymoron: a paradox operating at the level of a single phrase, as in "dim roar" (Wilde)

Passive: a past-participial format (the inverse of transitive grammar) in which the syntactic subject is the object or recipient of the action, often without stated "agent," as in the disembodied "the paper was read aloud" (Dickens) or a character being "hurried along in a new movement" (Eliot)

Parallelism: as one key manifestation of Jakobson's "poetic function," any marked recurrence across the structure of a passage (one level up, in diction or syntax, from alliteration or assonance – and less a strict repetition than anaphora)

Parataxis: the taxiing of meaning across a sentence operating either without the distance-keeping grammar of conjunctions (in the *comma splicing* of *run-on* clauses) or at least without clearly marked paths of subordination (*hypotaxis*), as in the syntactic cascade of "he was flat on his back on the beach in the freezing sand, and it was raining out of a low sky, and the tide was way out" (Wallace)

Participle (present): *ing* forms in a "progressive" grammar of the ongoing, used either adjectivally or verbally – or both together for extra momentum (Melville: "small fowls flew screaming over the yet yawning gulf"; Dickens: "clashing engines going at things unknown")

Participle (past): *ed* forms indicating completed action – and sometimes serving merely an adjectival role, as in the d- as well as g-heavy "grim haggard amazed" (Faulkner), where the passive agent of the amazement (by what or whom?) goes unsaid, as if pervasive

Periodic sentence: a phrasal format that interrupts the main syntactic arc of a clause with intermediate material, producing a kind of grammatical suspense, as with over half a dozen **absolute constructions** and subordinate clauses inserted by Dickens between the prepositional phrase "In the dead silence and stillness" and "the paper was read in court" – or, at narrower scale in James, a character "missing wholly, *though it now, to my sense, filled the room like the taste of poison,* the wide overwhelming presence"

Personification: the attribution of human qualities or agency to inanimate objects or conditions, as in "the figure-head" of a ship "making a speech to the winds" (Dickens)

Phoneme: smallest unit of discernible speech sound, forming the basis of syllables in semantic process, as in the repeated **plosive** consonant in "*bobb*ing *b*uoys ... shi*ps' b*oys" (Dickens) or the title vowels of an entire novel in further distribution when tracking a "w*o*rd thr*ou*gh the t*u*nneled *u*nderw*o*rld of its ancestr*a*l r*oo*ts" (DeLillo's *Underworld*)

Phonetic bracket: the consonant framework around an expanded vowel nucleus, as produced by various accordioned sound effects in a rhyme-like slant progression, as in the decline from manorial "*seat*" to "*sea-beat*en" exile (Scott) or "*ethereal thrill*" (Melville) or, with an overlapping effect, "*b*ird-girl gird*l*ed" (Ellison)

Pleonasm: phrasal redundancy, as in "swiftness and motion" (Wilde), related there to **hendiadys**

Plosive: forced-air consonant *b* or *p*, sometimes involved in a mimetic effect of pressure, explosion, or compaction, as in Dickens's **adjective chain** "a narrow lo*p*sided wooden jum*b*le of cor*p*ulent windows hea*p*ed one u*p*on another"

Poetic function (Jakobson): the semantically irrelevant iteration (rhyming) of phonetic, metrical, or other verbal forms that, in structuring a message, call attention to the messaging itself by just its self-conscious patterning (namely, its "projection of the principle of

equivalence from the axis of selection to the axis of combination");
Jakobson's famous example: "I Like Ike"

Prepositions (and their vectors): short parts of speech, usually preceding nouns, deployed to orient the predication in time or space (as when Robinson Crusoe maps his genealogical backstory as a matter of his parents being *of* and coming *from* and arriving *to*)

Pun: one word pattern, lexeme or phrase, taken in two ways at once, as in the sound of *cruise* in the shortened German name "Crusoe" (Defoe) or "trancemission" (Wallace); see also **homophone**

Sibilance: the recurrent buzz or hiss of *s, z,* or soft *c* sounds, sometimes liable to cross-word elisions, as in Melville's "concentric circles seized" (where a sinking ship's suction is felt in the sounds themselves)

Simile: a form of metaphoric language involving an explicit *as* or *like* comparison (Waugh: "ape-like") or sometimes overdone with two analogues at once, as in Fielding's "like a hungry tigress ... like a voracious pike"

Slant Rhyme: by analogy with effects in poetry, an oblique echo in which either the vowel or the consonant patterns (or both) of nearby syllables are matched, as in "*firm form*ality" and "clear*er* riv*er*" (Dickens)

Syllepsis: a "taking together" in divergent senses across two slightly different usages (regularly involving objects in divided relation to their predicate, often metaphoric versus literal), as in "torn from the London season and the indelicate advances of debutantes" (Waugh)

Synecdoche: a figure of speech in which part is substituted (metaphorically) for the whole, or whole for the part, as lurking behind Miéville's "I met her eyes," where in fact no interpersonal contact, no other "meeting," takes place

Synesthesia: the blending of sensory registers in description, as when color and taste idiomatically combine in "honey-sweet and honey-colored laburnums" (Wilde), or sound and image for "loud cloudy flutter" (Faulkner)

Telescoping (or collapsed bracket): the compression of syllabic matter from one word to another, as in "terror tore" (Wharton)

Transferred epithet: see **epithet**

Trope (a **"turning aside"**): the common name for a figure of speech (an "image" in the metaphoric sense), but one whose analogic service can also by rendered by some kind of syntactic enactment – in a grammar elongated or pivotal, for instance – as well as by a semantic "turn of phrase"

Vowel Nucleus: the core vowel sound of a word, often deployed by assonant repetition across the **phonetic bracket** of two or more lexemes, as in "gloom brooding" (Conrad)

Zeugma: from the Greek "yoking together," the forced conjunction of disparate senses in a compound phrase, as famously in Alexander Pope's "stain her honour, or her new brocade"; often interchangeable in designation with **syllepsis**

By closing with a roster of glosses that might have been relegated to an appendix, but is instead elevated to chapter status, what is suggested is that an enabling acquaintance with such terms, in full structural parity with previously investigated examples from prose fiction, should for some readers open a whole new chapter in the precision, and thus intensity, of literary response. The power of style's chosen words is that they often induce an itch for words of our own to account for them. Reading in this intimate sense bears with it an instilled desire for a kind of rewriting from within. The value of style, its profit, is in this way continuously reinvested at the level of verbal fascination itself, renewed from page to page by every fresh enthusiasm. What each is worth is up to you, to your own style of uptake.

Notes

I INTRODUCTION: VERBAL INVESTMENTS –
RICHNESS, WEALTH, VALUE

1. Peter Boxall, *The Value of the Novel* (New York, NY: Cambridge University Press, 2015).
2. Hayden White, *The Content of the Form: Narrative Discourse and Historical Representation* (Baltimore, MD: Johns Hopkins University Press, 1987).
3. Angela Leighton, *On Form: Poetry, Aestheticism, and the History of a Word* (Oxford: Oxford University Press, 2007). We have no similar history of the word "style." But there is no shortage of splendid attention to it in Susan Wolfson's *Formal Charges: The Shaping of Poetry in British Romanticism* (Stanford, CA: Stanford University Press, 1997) or D.A. Miller's *Jane Austen, or the Secret of Style* (Princeton, NJ: Princeton University Press, 2003).
4. As an early harbinger of a movement mostly eclipsed by the late-1960s, see the study of figurative subtexts in Mark Schorer, "Fiction and the 'Matrix of Analogy,'" *The Kenyon Review* Vol. 11, No. 4 (Autumn, 1949), pp. 539–60.
5. Terry Eagleton, *How to Read a Poem* (London: Wiley and Sons, 2007), 1.
6. Franco Moretti, "Network Theory, Plot Analysis," *New Left Review* Vol. 68 (March–April, 2011), 80–102.
7. Hugh Kenner, *The Mechanic Muse* (Oxford: Oxford University Press, 1987), 121.
8. Stanley Fish, *Surprised by Sin: The Reader in Paradise Lost* (Cambridge: Harvard University Press, 1967), its theoretical claims further elaborated in "Literature in the Reader: Affective Stylistics," *New Literary History* Vol. 2, No. 1 (Autumn, 1970), pp. 123–62.
9. Michael H. Short and Geoffrey N. Leech, *Style in Fiction: A Linguistic Introduction to English Fictional Prose* (Harlow: Pearson Education, Ltd., 1981).

10. That there is no necessary divorce between a cultural/historical/ political approach and the leverage offered by verbal attention is testified to in my extended reading of historicized racial politics in the pre-Revolutionary American setting of Toni Morrison's *A Mercy* (2008), turning as it does on the one appearance of the institutional word "slavery" only in the phonetic ambiguity of the heroine's climactic monologue, "Slave. Free. I'll last," with the phrasing's mordant overtone of "slavery'll last." See "Talking Room," the final chapter of Garrett Stewart, *The Deed of Reading: Literature • Writing • Language • Philosophy* (Ithaca, NY: Cornell University Press, 2015), 181–208.

11. Gordon Teskey, *The Poetry of John Milton* (Cambridge, MA: Harvard University Press, 2015), xiv.

12. Stephen Best and Sharon Marcus, "Surface Reading: An Introduction," special issue on "The Way We Read Now," *Representations* Vol. 108, No. 1 (Fall 2009), 1–22.

13. Garrett Stewart, *Reading Voices: Literature and the Phonotext* (Berkeley, CA: University of California Press, 1990).

14. David Nowell Smith, *On Voice in Poetry: The Work of Animation* (New York, NY: Palgrave Macmillan, 2015).

15. The title of Jameson's discipline-changing book, *The Political Unconscious* (Ithaca, NY: Cornell University Press, 1981), with its subtitle, *Narrative as a Socially Symbol Form*, giving equal weight to the formal as well as to the social and the symbolic. Steven Connor, *Beckett, Modernism, and the Material Imagination* (New York, NY: Cambridge University Press, 2014), Chapter 7, "In My Soul, I Suppose, Where the Acoustics Are So Bad: Writing the White Voice," 102–14.

16. John Mullan, "Style," *How Novels Work* (New York, NY: Oxford University Press, 2009), 213–50.

17. Fredric Jameson, *The Political Unconscious: Narrative as a Socially Symbolic Act* (Ithaca, NY: Cornell University Press, 1981).

18. Roland Barthes, *S/Z: An Essay* (New York, NY: Hill and Wang, 1971), trans. Richard Miller.

19. Barthes, "Voices" summarized in *S/Z*, 190–211.

20. Stewart, *The Deed of Reading: Literature • Writing • Language • Philosophy* (n. 10).

21. Barthes, "Myth Today," *Mythologies*, trans. Annette Lavers (New York, NY: Hill and Wang, 1970), 112.

22. David Bordwell, *Narration and the Fiction Film* (Madison, WI: University of Wisconsin Press, 1985), 55.

23. Roman Jakobson, "Linguistics and Poetics: Closing Statement," *Style in Language*, ed. Thomas E. Sebeok (New York, NY: Wiley, 1970), 358.

24. Joseph Conrad, *Heart of Darkness*, ed. Robert Kimbrough (New York, NY: W.W. Norton, 1988), 9.

25. Nathaniel Hawthorne, *The House of the Seven Gables* (New York, NY: Bantam, 1986), 207.

26. Madelyn Detloff, *The Value of Virginia Woolf* (New York, NY: Cambridge University Press, 2016), 1.

27. Charles Altieri, *Reckoning with the Imagination: Wittgenstein and the Aesthetics of Literary Experience* (Ithaca, NY: Cornell University Press, 2015), 12.

28. Virginia Woolf, *To the Lighthouse*, ed. Mark Hussey (New York, NY: Harcourt, 2005), 132.

29. The grammatical arc was originally and quite oddly broken off – as if left dramatically suspended – for the downbeat of a new extra sentence, as follows, inverting the initial placement of the adverbial phrase about the "dark" morning, yet this as the least of its syntactic eccentricities: ". . . stretched his arms out one dark morning, but, Mrs. Ramsay having died suddenly the night before, he stretched his arms out [as if to say "*merely* stretched them out"]. They remained empty." See "A Note on the Text," xxxv, *To the Lighthouse*, ed. Margaret Drabble (Oxford: Oxford World Classics, 1992), where the editor cites the phrasing this way in deference to Woolf's having never adjusted it for the official Hogarth Press edition. With the "but" logically as well as grammatically disjunctive, and the whole span less molded and rhythmic than in the American edition, including a tempting override of the comma at "the night before [,] he stretched his arms out," certainly any freeze-frame effect on that reiterated gesture of the unreciprocated reach is all the more jolting in this version.

30. See, for instance, Virginia Tufte, *Artful Sentences: Syntax as Style* (New York, NY: Graphics Press, 2006) and Brooks Landon, *Building Great Sentences: How to Write the Kinds of Sentences You Like to Read* (New York, NY: Plume, 2013), based on his "Great Courses" DVD set *Building Great Sentences: Exploring the Writer's Craft* (New York, NY: The Teaching Company, 2013).

31. This level of analytic affinity and participation is to be distinguished, not from his own gifted practice certainly, but only from what D. A. Miller, when referring specifically to free indirect discourse in *Jane Austen, or the Secret of Style*, calls "the fantasmatics of that technique of *close writing* that Austen more or less invented for the English novel" (58).

2   EMERGENT TURNS: DEFOE TOWARD DICKENS

1. Daniel Defoe, *The Adventures of Robinson Crusoe*, ed. John Richetti (New York, NY: Penguin, 2003), 5.
2. Charles Dickens, *Great Expectations*, ed. Charlotte Mitchell (New York, NY: Penguin, 2003), 3.
3. Laurence Sterne, *A Sentimental Journey through France and Italy*, ed. Gardner D. Stout, Jr. (Berkeley, CA: University of California Press, 1967), 201.
4. Henry Fielding, *Joseph Andrews*, ed. Martin C. Battestin (New York, NY: Houghton Mifflin, 1961), 8.
5. Charles Dickens, *Little Dorrit*, ed. Stephen Wall and Helen Small (New York, NY: Penguin, 1998), 18.
6. Walter Scott, *The Bride of Lammermoor* (London: ElecBook, 2000), 37.
7. Scott, *Ivanhoe*, ed. Graham Tulloch (New York, NY: Penguin, 2000), 17.
8. Charles Dickens, *The Pickwick Papers* (New York, NY: Modern Library, 2003), 3.
9. Jane Austen, *Pride and Prejudice* (Garden City, NY: Millennium, 2014), 44.
10. Miller, *Jane Austen, or the Secret of Style*.
11. Austen, *Persuasion*, ed. D.W. Harding (New York, NY: Penguin, 1987), 253.
12. Edgar Allan Poe, "MS. Found in a Bottle," *The Complete Tales and Poems of Edgar Allan Poe* (New York, NY: Random House, 1975), 120–1.
13. Poe, "The Oval Portrait," 290.
14. Poe, "The Fall of the House of Usher," 235.
15. Poe, "The Premature Burial," 264.
16. Poe, "The Masque of the Red Death," 270.
17. William Empson, *7 Types of Ambiguity* (New York, NY: New Directions, 1966), 48–57.
18. Conrad, *Heart of Darkness*, 3
19. Joseph Conrad, *The Arrow of Gold: A Story Between Two Notes* (Philadelphia, PA: University of Pennsylvania Press, 2004), 3.
20. Charles Dickens, *Dombey and Son*, ed. Andrew Sanders (New York, NY: Penguin, 2002), 431.
21. Dickens, *Great Expectations*, 436.

22. A more colorful version of this is Dickens coining a new verb for Pancks's detective work in *Little Dorrit*, where the industrious character explains "how he had felt his way inch by inch, and 'Moled it out, sir' (that was Mr Pancks's expression), grain by grain" (432).

23. "'The idea of coming along the open streets, in the broad light of day, with a *Pauper!*' (firing off the last word as if it were a ball from an air-gun)," in Dickens, *Little Dorrit*, 390.

3   STYLISTIC MICROPLOTS: MELVILLE TO MIÉVILLE

1. Herman Melville, *Moby Dick, or the Whale* (Berkeley, CA: University of California Press, 1979), 576.

2. Nathaniel Hawthorne, *The House of the Seven Gables* (New York, NY: Bantam, 1986), 207.

3. Charlotte Brontë, *Jane Eyre* (Ware, Hertfordshire: Wordsworth, 1999), 261.

4. Henry James, *The Turn of the Screw*, ed. Deborah Esch and Jonathan Warren (New York, NY: W. W. Norton, 1999), 85.

5. Robert Louis Stevenson, *The Strange Case of Dr. Jekyll and Mr. Hyde* (Mineola, NY: Dover, 1991), 47.

6. Walter Pater, *The Works of Walter Pater, Vol 1, The Renaissance: Studies in Art and Poetry* (Cambridge: Cambridge University Press, 2001), 236.

7. Oscar Wilde, *The Picture of Dorian Gray*, ed. Donald L. Lawler (New York, NY: W.W. Norton, 1988), 7.

8. John Ruskin, *The Stones of Venice*, Vol 2 (Boston, MA: Dana Estes, 1900), chap. III. iii, 32.

9. E. M. Forster, *Howards End*, ed. Oliver Stallybrass (New York, NY: Penguin, 1992), 61.

10. George Eliot, *The Mill on the Floss*, ed. A. S. Byatt (New York, NY: Penguin, 1985), 655.

11. George Eliot, *Middlemarch*, ed. Bert Hornbeck (New York, NY: W.W. Norton, 2000), 491

12. D. H. Lawrence, *Women in Love*, ed. David Farmer, Lyndeth Vasey, and John Worthen (Cambridge: Cambridge University Press, 1987), 369.

13. Kazuo Ishiguro, *Never Let Me Go* (Toronto: Knopf Canada, 2006), 263.

14. China Miéville, *The City & the City* (New York, NY: Ballantine, 2009), 312.

4 A RHETORICAL SPECTRUM: WHARTON, WOOLF, WAUGH, WALLACE, AND BEYOND

1. Edith Wharton, *The House of Mirth* (New York, NY: Signet Classics, 2015), 335.
2. Virginia Woolf, *Mrs. Dalloway* (New York, NY: Harvest, 1953), 5.
3. William Wordsworth, "Tintern Abbey," *William Wordsworth: the Major Works*, ed. Stephen Gill (New York, NY: Oxford University Press, 1984), 133, l. 49.
4. Evelyn Waugh, *A Handful of Dust & Decline and Fall* (New York, NY: Dell, 1970), 278.
5. John Steinbeck, *The Grapes of Wrath* (New York, NY: Penguin, 2006), 196.
6. Dickens, *Little Dorrit*, 386.
7. Dickens, *Our Mutual Friend*, ed. Adrian Poole (New York, NY: Penguin, 1997), 21.
8. Dickens, *Great Expectations*, 3.
9. Mark Twain, *Adventures of Huckleberry Finn* (New York, NY: Dover, 1994), 1.
10. William Faulkner, *Absalom, Absalom!* (New York, NY: New American Library, 1951), 7.
11. Thomas Pynchon, *Mason & Dixon* (New York, NY: Henry Holt), 106.
12. Cormac McCarthy, *Blood Meridian: Or the Evening Redness in the West* (New York, NY: Modern Library, 2001), 45.
13. Lee Clark Mitchell, *Mere Reading: the Poetics of Wonder in Modern American Novels* (New York, NY: Bloomsbury, 2017).
14. Vladimir Nabokov, *The Annotated Lolita: Revised and Updated*, ed. Alfred Appel, Jr. (New York, NY: Vintage, 1991), 98.
15. James Joyce, *Finnegans Wake* (New York, NY: Penguin, 1976), 258:21.
16. Ralph Ellison, *Invisible Man* (New York, NY: Vintage, 1950), 19.
17. Toni Morrison, *Beloved* (New York, NY: Vintage, 1987), xix.
18. Don DeLillo, *Falling Man* (New York, NY: Scribner, 2007), 246.
19. DeLillo, 1993 interview: www.theparisreview.org/interviews/1887/don-delillo-the-art-of-fiction-no-135-don-delillo.

20. Dickens, *Little Dorrit*, 69.
21. John Mullan, *How Novels Work* (New York, NY: Oxford University Press, 2006), 223, quoting *Underworld*, 223.
22. Don DeLillo, *Underworld* (New York, NY: Scribner, 1997), 415.
23. I. A. Richards, *Principles of Literary Criticism* (New York, NY: Routledge, 2001), vii.

Index